lifesaving

Also by Judith Barrington

Poetry
TRYING TO BE AN HONEST WOMAN
HISTORY AND GEOGRAPHY

Nonfiction
WRITING THE MEMOIR: FROM TRUTH TO ART

lifesaving

a memoir

Judith Barrington

THE EIGHTH MOUNTAIN PRESS

PORTLAND ◆ OREGON ◆ 2000

Cover and book design: Marcia Barrentine

Cover art: *La Riera* by Joan Barrington, and photographs used by permission of Judith Barrington.

First American Edition, 2000

1 2 3 4 5 6 7 8 9

Printed in the United States on acid-free paper.

Some of the chapters in *Lifesaving* were previously published as follows:

"Umbilical" in *The American Voice;* "No Escape," (an earlier version titled "Worlds Apart") in *An Inn Near Kyoto: Writing by American Women Abroad,* edited by Kathleen Coskran and C.W. Truesdale, New Rivers Press, 1998; "The Road to Perelada," (an earlier version titled "Of Catalans and Kings") in *The House on Via Gombito: Writing by American Women Abroad,* edited by Madelon Sprengnether and C.W. Truesdale, New Rivers Press, 1991; "The Initiation" in *Left Bank;* "Paco's Mother" in The *Women's Review of Books;* "Sleeping Around" in *The Sonora Review* (Nonfiction Annual Award).

"He Wishes for the Cloths of Heaven" by William Butler Yeats, from *The Wind Among the Reeds* (1899).

LIBRARY OF CONGRESS CATALOGING-IN-PUBLICATION DATA
Barrington, Judith.
    Lifesaving : a memoir / Judith Barrington. -- 1st American ed.
      p. cm.
    1. Barrington, Judith. 2. Parents--Death--Psychological aspects.
    3. Poets, American--20th century--Biography. 4. Poets, English--
    20th century--Biography. 5. Lesbians--Spain--Biography. I. Title.

    PS3552.A73647 Z466 2000
    811'.54--dc21
    [B]   99-046447

The Eighth Mountain Press
624 Southeast 29th Avenue, Portland, Oregon 97214
phone: 503/233-3936 *fax:* 503/233-0774

table of contents

acknowledgments

I could not have completed this book without the encouragement and invaluable advice of many friends. I am extremely grateful to Ursula K. Le Guin, Andrea Carlisle, Barbara Wilson, and Martha Gies, who read the whole manuscript at various stages of its life. Thanks, too, to Molly Gloss, Sandy Dorr, Valerie Miner, John Daniel, Jeannette Doob, Katharine Salzmann, and Willa Schneberg for their careful readings and thoughtful comments.

The writing of this memoir was supported by grants from The Oregon Arts Commission and Literary Arts, Inc., for which I am very grateful. Residencies at Hedgebrook and at the Tyrone Guthrie Centre in Ireland gave me valuable time with the work. Many thanks for the use of the Multnomah County Library's Sterling Writers' Room.

For her brilliant insights and careful work with the text, I am especially indebted to my editor, Ruth Gundle, without whose loving support I could never have brought my story this far.

Please note that I have used the Spanish names for the places in Catalonia mentioned in this book. In the years during which the events described here took place, their Catalan names were not generally used. Only after the Franco years was the Catalan brought back into widespread use and printed on maps and on the signs for towns and villages.

PROLOGUE

Umbilical

I MUST HAVE BEEN TWELVE when my father, my mother, and I participated in the Shoreham to Littlehampton yacht race. Actually, I did that race more than once, but I'm talking about the only time my mother came along—the time that turned into full-blown family story.

The way I see it, the story is about my mother's lifelong terror of the sea and my father's pigheadedness. Or perhaps it is about the absurd pretenses of the British middle class, particularly the male of that species, whose dignity must be preserved at all costs. It might be in part about those costs—about the price some of us paid for keeping up that pretense. It might, too, be about a child's lifelong yearning to save her mother. Inevitably, though, as I set out to tell what happened on the day of the race, the telling is also about the creation of myth and the fallibility of memory. Memory lurking in the shadow of myth, waiting to be lost in the dark.

It should have been an easy day's sail: straight down the river from the yacht club, through the harbor where the ocean swell starts to lift, right past the harbor wall, the marker boat and the starting gun, and then a straight run west to Littlehampton. But the trouble began early that morning even before we cast off from our mooring out in the current of the river. My mother, strangely quiet and afraid of getting seasick, disregarded all instructions as my father and I handed her down from the jetty into the little dinghy to row out to the sailboat. Avoiding the floorboards, she stepped firmly on to blue canvas, causing the collapsible dinghy to collapse, folding up around her legs and dragging her down into the mud.

While she drove home to get dry clothes I wondered if she would return. She had been complaining about this trip for days, reciting an inventory of things she had to do and pointing out the silliness of going to all that trouble just to race a few miles along a straight coastline. Anyway, she had said more than once, Littlehampton was a place no one in their right mind would go to spend the night. I knew that all this covered up a genuine terror—I knew it because she had once told me she would certainly die at sea and I had believed her. I can't remember now where or why she told me this crucial fact, but I do remember subsequent evidence for the truth of her claim: how she had to leave the cinema when the storm-at-sea came on; how she always turned pale on the most tranquil crossing of the car ferry from Dover to Calais. I would hardly have blamed her if she had used the dinghy accident as an excuse to opt out of the Littlehampton race that day, but some sense of honor, or perhaps some unspoken threat on the part of my father, brought her back an hour later, and we cast off in time to catch the start of the race.

Chugging down the river under power, I watched my mother blanch as the smell of gas wafted up from the inboard motor. Turning away, I tried to ignore the brilliant yellow paint with which my father had insisted on covering the twenty-eight-foot sailboat he had named *Guapa*, Spanish for pretty. I did not find his yellow at all pretty—had, indeed, wanted midnight blue, which was my current color. My mother, the earth-loving gardener, had voted for green. But my father, anxious to show off his few gleanings of nautical knowledge, insisted on yellow, which, he said, was the most visible color at sea. Hence yellow lifejackets. Being at that stage of hating my father—a stage that lasted a long time—I sat there glaring at the gleaming yellow paint and feeling embarrassed as I did almost all the time, particularly around my parents. If yellow were safer, then all yachts would be painted yellow. But there was not a single one at the yacht club or anywhere on the river. No one else was crass enough to sail in something that looked like a floating egg yolk.

Once clear of the harbor wall, we hoisted our sails and set off towards Worthing. Pretty soon the wind dropped to a faint breath, so we hauled in the foresail and replaced it with the larger genoa, trying to keep up with three or four racier yachts that were hoisting spinnakers. Without the motor's noise and smell, my mother had cheered up a bit but sat very still next to my father, who held the tiller and stared eagerly ahead. When I wasn't being yelled at to haul a sheet or prepare to tack, I lay on the cabin top, staring up past the mast to the heavily clouded sky that occasionally flashed a patch of blue. Ahead in the distance Worthing pier reached out from the land, its as yet invisible tourists strolling high above the oily water with pink candyfloss in sticky hands, and the old people, who made up most of Worthing's population, sitting elbow to elbow in striped deck chairs. Here there was nothing but the sheets snapping rhythmically against the metal mast, the dark green water rolling under us with an occasional slap, and the sea gulls mewing as they veered away again and again.

Some time later I went into the cabin to get a sweater. The clouds seemed lower and my father was tapping his new gimbal-mounted compass. When I came back up we were in a thick mist: there was no sign of the pier. Looking towards the beach, I realized that had gone too. As had the wind. Drops of water collected in my hair as my father started up the motor and chugged a little out to sea. "We'll give the pier a good wide berth," he said. My mother sat rigid, her hands clenched, and said nothing.

An hour later, I was sitting right up on the bow eating potato chips out of the packet, having figured that my mother, who was beginning to look green, wouldn't want to be around them. The swell had flattened out, the fog now so thick it blurred even my father at the tiller. I was hating him again as the motor popped along healthily, interrupted by his cheerful, shouted comments: "Good thing I brought plenty of fuel," or, "Won't take too long at this rate." From time to time he leaned forward to the new compass and spun it around, or contemplated it with his head to one side. I knew he had no idea how it worked.

Pretty soon it started to seem as if we were not moving at all with no land by which to measure our progress and the turgid water hardly reacting to our forward motion. Just when it seemed we might chug along forever in one spot, there was a substantial bump followed by unmistakable forward motion as we ground onto a rock.

"What is it? What's happened?" said my mother in a high-pitched, barely controlled voice.

"We've hit a rock," said my father, after he had shut off the motor. "We've hit a rock."

"Well of course I know that," said my mother in the scathing tones I knew covered her panic. "I'm not entirely bereft of wits, even after this abysmal morning. What I mean is, what are you going to do about it?"

My father looked flustered. He stood up, then sat down again. Then, with an air of decision, he stood up and shrugged his body as he often did when setting off on a mission. He headed down into the cabin and spread out a chart on the table. "I'm looking for the rock," he called up to us as we peered down in disbelief.

"Oh don't be so silly, Rex," my mother snapped. "What good will that do. It's clearly a rock and we're clearly stuck on it. It doesn't matter where it is. Just get us off it." For a moment her chin trembled as it did when she was going to cry. I had only seen that twice in my life. My father missed it altogether.

"Well," said my father, "if the tide isn't still going out, we can probably pull her off." And he got out the dinghy, uncollapsed it again, attached it to a long rope, and put the anchor in it. Then he said I should get in and row away from the stern until he told me to stop and drop the anchor.

I wasn't more than ten yards out when the fog swallowed me up. I was in my own grey world unattached to anything except the rope that stretched away like a long umbilical cord towards my parents' voices, which were getting dangerously loud. "Get her back here at once," my mother was saying, a slight tremor under the anger in her voice. "I won't have it, I say." Pretty soon my father was yelling too. "For God's sake, Violet, shut up and stop overreacting. The girl's perfectly safe: she's attached by this rope, can't you see?"

I rowed on steadily, wondering if I was dreaming, wondering if I would ever have to go back to the yacht or if I could just sit here in this soft patch of cotton wool until the voices faded into silence. With a gleeful flash of anger, I noted that I couldn't see *Guapa* through the fog even with her yellow paint. So much for that theory! Then, just when I was returning to a pleasurable sort of limbo, my father shouted out to me to drop the anchor.

When I was safely back on board he started the motor and threw it into reverse while we all three pulled on the anchor rope, trying to haul *Guapa* off her rocky bed, but she wouldn't budge. "I suppose the tide is still going out," he said. "We'll just have to stay here till it comes back in and lifts us off."

"And just how long will that be?" demanded my mother.

"Oh, only a few hours," he said airily.

My mother and I looked at each other. He didn't know.

SEVEN years later both my parents drowned. It wasn't obviously my father who bungled it that time, unless you consider persuading, even coercing, a person terrified of the sea into taking a cruise to be a bungle. It was, after all, the ship's owners who fudged the proper inspections and sent the cruise ship *Lakonia* to sea with a rewiring job that would start a fire; it was the ship's crew who panicked and lowered the lifeboats so that several capsized, and the ship's captain who allowed the remaining lifeboats to leave only half filled. Yet, 905 passengers did manage to get rescued, while my parents were among only

131 who drowned. There was room in there for some bungling, and I couldn't help wondering: was it simply chance or had there been crucial choices to make? Were there disagreements between my parents?—it was easy to imagine my mother simply refusing to get into one of those lifeboats after hearing the screams of those pitched into the sea. And had my father pretended to know more than he actually did, even to the bitter end, when finally they were forced to climb down the ladder from the burning ship into the sea?

I know too little to tell the story of what happened on that cruise ship, so I continue to tell the other story, the funny one. It is a story that has been told so many times by so many different members of my family that the facts are clear, though possibly not accurate. But in spite of the repetitions that move the story away from actual recall, I can still feel the clammy fog on my face and see the drops of water rolling down the yellow paint. And although it's a stretch, I can see my parents, too: Pa in his blue beret, looking absurdly unlike either a French fisherman or a painter; looking, in fact, as if he should be wearing the blue blazer with brass buttons worn by all those other amateur yachtsmen—the ones I imagined were drinking whiskey in Littlehampton while we sat on our rock somewhere off the south coast of England. And my mother? Well, I remember the bulkiness of her cold, hunched figure and the anxious look that furrowed her face between the eyebrows—the furrow that deepened when we started to hear the foghorns of the big ships. I remember the bodily shape of her worry, the worry that never failed to stir up a panic in my stomach and make me want to save her from it all.

What I can't capture is the daughter. The twelve-year-old with the sulky expression who dragged her feet annoyingly against the grainy cabin top when asked to go to the bow and look out. It can hardly have been simple hatred for her father that sustained her, yet that is all I remember. There must have been something else back then, but the anger is all that remained—the only memory that survived seven years later when the father, once again, took the mother to sea. When the daughter wasn't there to save anyone.

THE foghorns were really unnerving. We all knew there were major shipping lanes up and down the English Channel and my mother and I, confident that my father had no idea of how to work the compass, realized we could have been heading straight out to sea ever since we lost sight of the shore. It was hard not to imagine the prow of an oil tanker looming up like a great cliff out of the fog and smashing us to pieces. The only comfort was the rock. "All ships must know about this rock," my father said when finally he caught on to our fear. "They'll be steering well clear of us."

"Yeah, if they know how to work their compasses," I muttered under my breath.

From time to time my mother and I played a game. "I spy" was not a success since we could spy nothing beyond the little well where the three of us sat, unwilling to go below and give up the illusion of participating in our fate. But "twenty questions" moved along lethargically until we failed to agree on whether the rock underneath our keel was mineral as my mother presumed or animal, according to my unlikely claim that it might be a coral reef or a pile of mussel shells. Tapping out the rhythms of tunes from musicals went well for a while, but my father, who was as unmusical as anyone could be, clearly found it annoying. Finally when I was giving a fine two-handed rendition on the cabin roof of "The Surrey with the Fringe on Top," he said, "Oh, do stop that noise Judith. I'm trying to listen for the tide to turn," so I stopped and went below to read the old stained Sherlock Holmes paperback that had lived in one of the lockers ever since my first overnight voyage in *Guapa*.

I was down there reading when I heard my mother say in a tense voice, "What's that?"

"What's what?" said my father. "Where?"

"There. There. To the right of the mast. See?"

I came up the steps and stared into the fog. There did seem to be a blurry form: perhaps a sea gull, though it wasn't moving much. I focused on it as if it were twenty or thirty yards away, assuming it was not a ship or a sailboat. Could there be a marker buoy out here?

Suddenly, shockingly, the dark mass organized itself into a human figure. A dog ran barking out of the white void. A man was walking his dog less than twenty feet away on smooth sand. We were all struck silent for a minute, even my father. Then the man waved. "Ahoy there," he said cheerfully.

My father pulled himself together. "Good afternoon," he said, almost standing to attention. "I say, would you mind telling us where we are—this fog's got us a bit confused you know."

"Oh dear," said the man. "This is Angmering beach. You know where that is?"

"Certainly," said my father. "But exactly which way is Littlehampton from here?"

I should have burst out laughing at this point. Perhaps I did. Maybe my mother, too, chuckled into her raincoat. But that's the trouble with memory. The laughing twelve-year-old, who might have had a fondness for her father's absurdity, has given way to the angry daughter of the pigheaded father. The much-told story—or perhaps the untold later story—has swallowed up the real memory.

"Well," said the man kindly, "it's straight along this way," and he pointed back the way he had come. "But it'll be a couple of hours before you've got enough water to float off there I should think. Can I do anything to help?"

"Oh no thanks, old chap," said my father. "We're fine. Damn nuisance though, this fog." And the man wandered off into his life, which presumably lurked out there just beyond our vision.

WE ended up spending the night aboard *Guapa*, anchored right outside Littlehampton harbor, it being too dark and foggy to find the buoys that marked the channel between the sand-banks. We had, indeed, floated off the rock as the tide came in, and discovered that no damage was done to the boat's bottom. Still, trying to sleep out there with the foghorns wailing and the night passing so slowly it might have been the whole sum-mer vacation, was definitely worse than sitting on the rock had been. We were much closer to the shipping lanes than we had been on Angmering beach.

My father slept. In fact he snored much of the night. When he was not sleeping he lay with one arm folded behind his head, apparently thinking. Would it help if I knew now what he was thinking back then? Would it dispel or merely fan the anger? Would it help piece together the second story—the story of that other ship, *Lakonia*, on that other dark night?

My mother lay quietly but did not sleep, her thoughts per-haps a rehearsal for the big event. Seven years later, some-where north of the Canary Isles, once again she would have too much time to wait and to think, surrounded by the ocean she had always known would get her in the end.

And what of me? I recall some facts: how my father never said "don't worry" to my mother except in an irritated way that really meant "shut up," and how my mother never once put her arms around me. Nobody admitted we were in danger. Nobody acknowledged any fear. Nobody acted as if it were out of the ordinary to be sleeping somewhere outside Littlehampton harbor. But feelings are more elusive than facts. Hard as it is now to see that twelve-year-old hugging her knees in her bunk or staring out of the porthole at the glint of water, I do know she wished she could do something heroic to save her mother. Usually she only had those feelings when her father was absent, and he was anything but absent here. He was supposed to be the hero, she reminded herself. Clearly it was his job to save her mother—and to the extent that the morning dawned clear and sunny, that they entered the harbor to discover that everyone else had given up and gone home leaving them to win the race, and that they ate one of the best breakfasts of their lives, she had to admit that he had, entirely by luck, managed to do his job. This time.

But seven years later, when someone—and she always knew in her heart of hearts that it was her father—really bungled it and there was no breakfast to be had in Littlehampton or anywhere else, then the twelve-year-old, who was by then a nineteen-year-old, knew that it had been her job all along. There was no doubt in her mind that she should have been there.

PART ONE

$\mathcal{N}o$ $\mathcal{E}scape$

 HELICOPTERS CIRCLED OVER-
head, but because of the
heat and thick smoke, they
could not get close enough to
lift off those stranded on
board after the lifeboats had
left. A whole fleet of ships
gathered nearby but stayed at a distance because the water was
crowded with people drifting in leaky boats, clinging to pieces
of furniture, or floating in their lifejackets amidst the charred
wreckage. The world watched television pictures of the ship
dragging its pall of smoke across the Atlantic until, just before
dawn, all the remaining passengers climbed down a rope ladder into the sea. When my parents' bodies were picked up by
a British naval ship, they were taken to Gibraltar, where they
were buried alongside a dozen or so other British and German
passengers.

A few months earlier, in the fall of 1963, I had left home and settled into a rambling apartment in Kensington, which I shared with three other young women. I still went home nearly every weekend with my dirty laundry and stories of my new job at the BBC and of the escalating circle of acquaintances I claimed as friends. Playing at being independent, at nineteen I had not yet become proficient at the game, and my parents seemed quite content to give me time. They had bailed me out when my paycheck ran out; they had picked me up at the station on Friday nights and dropped me off again on Sundays, when I returned to my London life refreshed by a weekend of sleep and cooked food—both rare commodities in the Kensington flat.

My brother and sister, fifteen and eleven years older than I, had long since cut the ties I still relied on. Married and with young children, they visited our parents in Brighton on an occasional Sunday, but the two families rarely came at the same time. We had never gone in for large family gatherings, and I suspect that no one liked having all the small children under one roof for too long.

That winter, there had been a number of arguments about where we would all gather for the holiday. Usually my mother made the turkey and Christmas pudding, but this year my sister, Ruth, or it might have been my brother, John—I'm not sure—balked at having the gathering at our parents' house. There were a number of tense telephone conversations and then a definite note of defiance when my parents announced that they would be gone over Christmas (and therefore no one would have to consider them). For my part, I hardly cared. The season produced an exciting stack of invitations to parties, some from people whose names I didn't even recognize, and I was planning to stay in London for as much of it as I could get away with—which is why, on Christmas Eve, I was in Regent Street having my hair cut when John tracked me down and telephoned to say the ship was on fire.

Later, I remembered that I had seen the news as I hurried along Piccadilly to that hair appointment: Cruise ship *Lakonia* on fire! scrawled across the *Evening Standard* vendors' billboards, and bellowed out in the bored, singsong tones of the phrase shouted a thousand times. But I had paid no attention, not even knowing the name of the ship my parents had chosen.

"What ship?" I asked stupidly, when he announced the news.

"The cruise ship," he repeated, while I leaned on the hairdresser's counter, staring at cans of hairspray in the glass case. "The one Ma and Pa are on. You'd better come down here tonight. The others are on their way."

We settled in to call the Greek Line office every hour, each taking our turn in the stuffy little cupboard under the stairs to listen to the recorded list of names—names of the living snatched from the sea and names of the dead hauled in and identified. Under the sloping ceiling, where the numbers of baby-sitters and repair services were scrawled in pencil on the crumbling plaster, I stood in my ragged blue sweater in the chilly afternoon, or in flannel pajamas in the middle of the night. The tape didn't start at A every time: we cut into it wherever it happened to be when the connection was made. Sometimes we had to start at C or D and go all the way around to B to find out that neither my mother nor my father had been added since our last call. In between, we went ahead with Christmas for the children: presents under the tree, turkey and Christmas pud, and an afternoon pantomime—was it Dick

Whittington?—on the 26th, all with the alphabetical lists running through our heads like a mantra. Sometimes, as we gathered to listen to the news and heard how the ship was belching black smoke into the air, we laughed about how our father would fix up a raft if nothing else was available. Once, my sister called my mother's house cleaner and told her to put blankets in the airing cupboard to warm.

One of those days, I stood by the window in the spare bedroom, looking out on to the frost-covered lawn where sparrows fought over the remains of some pie crust. I heard the door open and John come in. I heard him clear his throat and say, "They've found Pa. Picked him up. He's dead." Then I heard the door close and waited for him to come over beside me. I felt cold and white like the frost, but somewhere inside me a hint of warmth flickered towards my brother, waiting for him to be there with me. I would lean slightly into him. My head would touch his shoulder.

In a little while I turned away from the window. The room was empty. The sound of the door closing had been the sound of John leaving. I'll manage; I'll take care of myself, I would have thought, if thinking had been possible. But my brain was icy cold and the small warm spot inside had frozen up.

After the holiday I went back to my flat and to work. There was still no news of my mother although many bodies had been picked up and remained unidentified. These were mostly women since men usually carried wallets. John flew to Gibraltar and found my mother's body, leaving without telling me and arranging for our parents to be buried there on the Rock. If I had been asked, I would probably have said, "I don't care; do whatever you think."

On a blustery January day, we gathered at the little church

in Patcham where my mother had attended occasional Sunday morning services. There were no coffins—just a lot of people looking solemn and my sister crying. Not me: I was still frozen by the spare room window. I wouldn't cry for more than a year and then it would be only a small thaw followed by a much longer freeze. The church echoed as we sang, *Oh hear us when we cry to Thee for those in peril on the sea*—always one of my favorite hymns for its excellent tune. Bundled up in my good overcoat, I sang defiantly, ignoring Ruth's surprising sobs.

Later that month an official-looking letter arrived in an envelope embossed with a blue crest. Inside was a letter from the captain of the *Centaur*, which had picked up Ma and Pa's bodies. After expressing sympathy for my loss, the captain wrote that a few personal effects would be returned shortly. "And," he added, "I thought you might like to know that the wristwatches of both your parents had stopped at 6:12 a.m., indicating that they both went into the sea at the same time." I crumpled up the letter and threw it away.

By the end of March, Ruth and I had packed up our parents' house and sold the furniture. I had stoically acknowledged hundreds of sympathy letters, and, for £1000, signed away my right to sue the Greek Line, all with a robotlike efficiency. In April I started a secret affair with a woman and quit my job at the BBC. I wasn't talking to anyone about anything real; in fact, I was learning very quickly how to lie effectively. And then in May I was offered a summer job in Spain, which I accepted. I was on the run, leaving England to escape from grief, but heading, nonetheless, straight for the place where my parents had spent their happiest years together.

* * *

I CELEBRATED my twentieth birthday with a sumptuous French lunch at an open-air restaurant somewhere in the middle of the windswept plain south of Narbonne, accompanied by a good-looking hitchhiker named Tony. After paté, salade niçoise, and grilled trout stuffed with basil, I unloaded a large pile of gifts from the trunk of my Triumph Herald convertible, newly inherited from my mother. As I opened the parcels at the café table, ripping off the wrapping paper, Tony toasted me with champagne and sang a full round of the birthday song between each present. Hot gusts of wind tugged at the paper tablecloth and snatched a piece of shiny gold wrapping paper, tossing it away across the barren landscape until it caught on the spike of a prickly pear, where it struggled for a moment before freeing itself and sailing on only to become wedged in the twisted trunk of one lone olive tree, bent double by years of mistral.

Tony had materialized the day before, as I roared through Montauban with the top down. When I found myself stopped by a red light right next to where he stood hitching a ride, he asked very politely if I was going south. "Yes," I had said coldly, not inviting him in.

"Would you consider giving me a lift?" he said, in a north country accent, with no hint of a come-on. "I'd really be very grateful."

"All right then," I said ungraciously, and he swung his small suitcase into the back seat and hopped over the door to sit beside me. That night we'd found a cheap hotel, and taken two single rooms with no discussion. After dinner, which Tony paid for, he excused himself, pausing only to ask, "Is it all right for me to ride with you tomorrow as far as the frontier?"

32

"Sure," I'd said and meant it. I was getting used to him by then.

He was a perfect birthday companion, entering joyfully into the occasion in spite of having known me for only twenty-two hours. I had been unwilling to open my presents before I left England, but dragged them along, perhaps as a rather desperate way of staying in touch with the life I was leaving behind. Pushing aside dessert and coffee, I displayed the gifts on our small, round table, telling Tony about the people who had picked them out for me. There were records and bottles of perfume from my London friends, with whom I had partied, shaking the floors of shared flats to the beat of the Beatles. Tony laughed when I told him how my downstairs neighbors had called the police because of the noise, and how the policemen had taken off their helmets and danced with us till dawn. There was Elizabeth Arden hand cream from my old school friend Sue. Tony listened patiently as I told him how we used to cram for the summer exams on Sue's back patio, her mother begging us to turn down the little yellow transistor radio that blared out top twenty hits while we sang along, substituting the words of Shakespeare plays and biology texts for the lyrics. There were books from my brother and sister, and drawings and specially made cards from my niece and nephews, whose names Tony was quick to master.

But there was one part of my life I was not about to mention to Tony or anyone else, though I had felt compelled to drag it along, too, in the form of a small, lavender-wrapped gift. Many times since April, I had driven very fast for ten or eleven hours through the darkness, winding along beside roaring Welsh rivers, to spend a night with Sophia, the woman I had gone to for comfort after my parents died—the woman who by Easter had become my lover. And here, as I tore off the lavender paper, was her offering. It was a copy of *Spoon River*, inscribed on the flyleaf with a message that quoted in full the poem she had read to me one spring night in front of the fire. I read the first few words, *Had I the heavens' embroidered cloths...*, and snapped the book shut. Most of the time this part of my life remained hidden even from me. But here it was, nudging me into a guilty secrecy when Tony asked who the book was from. I blushed and shrugged, shoving it under a pile of wrapping paper, and left his question hanging in the dense air.

After lunch, sleepy and hot, we drove on towards the Spanish border, the wind whipping round the windshield, my silk scarf flapping wildly. As we sped across the parched land, Tony's head fell back and he dozed fitfully, while I seemed to float above, looking down at myself as if I were a character in a movie. I saw myself speeding across the brown plain in the sage green Triumph—a potent symbol of my mother, whose frustrated dreams and longing for adventure had become focused on having a convertible of her own. My father had, for years, made fun of this dream. He said that convertibles were impractical, especially in England, where you could rarely have the top down, and where the canvas roof leaked in winter. I thought he would never give in, but my mother had finally prevailed.

I liked the dashing figure I became in her little sports car, which was now mine. Only I knew its history and I wasn't telling. I hadn't shed a tear in the six months since my parents' deaths. I had drunk a lot of whiskey. I had stopped menstruating—but I wasn't thinking about that. Nor was I thinking about my parents. I was heading south with a suitcase full of new beachwear, a young woman without a care in the world.

Glancing sideways at Tony, whose head had now fallen forward as he snored gently into his chest, I felt myself smile indulgently. It was a smile that went with the whole picture—part of the role I was playing in this movie. For a few years now I had been confused about my relationships with men. Although I was good-looking enough to attract their interest, I had no idea how to talk to them. In fact, I had quite surprised myself at lunch, babbling about my life to Tony—but that was probably the champagne. Since the unmentionable love affair with Sophia had started, I had renewed my efforts toward men quite vigorously. I certainly hadn't yet approached the terrifying thought that I might be emotionally or sexually more tuned in to women, in spite of that Yeats poem inscribed in the book I had just unwrapped, the poem that played away in the recesses of my mind, conjuring shame and longing, and flashing images of skin and the heat of a fire:

Had I the heavens' embroidered cloths,
Enwrought with golden and silver light,
The blue and the dim and the dark cloths
Of night and light and the half-light,
I would spread the cloths under your feet:
But I, being poor, have only my dreams;
I have spread my dreams under your feet;
Tread softly because you tread on my dreams.

If there was a touch of desperation in the energy I directed at the opposite sex, it did not mean I couldn't like them; Tony, for example, was very likeable: I appreciated his droll jokes and his descriptions of life on his father's farm.

With the past securely packed back into the trunk, I was ready to contemplate the future. I was on my way to Spain, where I had a job waiting for me. Or so I believed. My brother had made snide comments about what he called the "white slave trade," insisting that I was out of my mind to go off alone without even a letter to confirm my appointment. Admittedly, the hiring had been a bit unusual: I had been introduced to Arturo Suqué by a man I was working for as a temporary secretary. Arturo was the son-in-law of one of the richest men in Spain, Don Miguel Mateu, whose many interests included the Cavas del Ampurdán, producers of Perelada wines. Arturo was looking for someone to take charge of the hordes of tourists who stopped by, wanting to visit the castle and the wine cellars. He thought Perelada, like many French vineyards, could use its history to advantage. Someone could live in the nearby town of Figueras and become the public relations person, interpreter, tour guide, and host to the major British wine importers. My fairly adequate Spanish, learned on many holidays in Spain with my parents, as well as at school, together with my boss's recommendation, got me the job.

Arturo had pressed some large bills into my hand at the end of our lunch meeting and asked, "When can you leave?"

"Beginning of next month," I had replied, pocketing the money. And that was that.

Now, as Tony woke up and shook his head, I stared at the breathtaking views that were unfolding in all directions, with the green Mediterranean glinting off to our left. After climbing towards Cerbère and the border post, we stopped high up over the turquoise sea and gazed south into Spain, past Port-Bou to a rocky headland that jutted out with a small fishing village nestled in its armpit—a headland that I would soon come to know well, as I raced over the road from Figueras to Rosas or Cadaqués. It was bare of trees, except for a few small olive groves, and loomed high against the deep blue sky.

Although the rugged landscape looked very similar to the north and to the south, and though I knew Catalonia spanned this French/Spanish frontier, I couldn't help imagining that everything would change just a few miles down the road as I stepped into Spain.

"I'll be leaving you at the frontier," Tony said after a long, companionable silence, and for a moment I found myself a little sad.

"Okay," I said casually. He was only a hitchhiker after all. Then, watching the sun flash on the waves below, I added, "Send a postcard if you like."

"I will," he said smiling. But he never did.

A couple of hours later, I turned left off the main highway, bumped down a dark, cobbled street, and emerged into the bustling square of Figueras. I circled the square till I found a parking place that seemed legal and climbed out, stretching cramped muscles. Everywhere I looked there was activity. Hundreds of people strolled up and down the *rambla* under a canopy of sycamores; waiters ran around the tables that lined the sidewalk, trays held high above their heads, starched white cloths tucked into the waists of their black trousers, accentuating narrow hips; children played in the dust, screaming at each other while their mothers screamed at them; traffic rumbled by, and even the birds seemed raucously argumentative.

Later this scene became so familiar that it was almost invisible. It was hard then to recapture this first impression: how foreign yet how comfortable it all seemed. How much I was an outsider, yet how immediately I knew I belonged. Leaving England had meant leaving the place where I had once fit, but where now, marked by loss, and perhaps also by my unthinkable attraction to women, I had become utterly different from everyone I knew. Here I was different too, but being foreign was a kind of difference I could manage and even enjoy.

I walked across the square and sat down at a table on the sidewalk, people staring at me from all sides and, as I sipped my first *café con leche* in Figueras, I wrapped this new culture like a blanket around my thin skin. The trees spread their protective foliage overhead. The cobbled streets spilled from the darkness on all sides into this pool of light and life. Had I been asked why I had come here, I would not have known how to answer.

I wasn't thinking about my mother—about the way she turned up her face and hands towards the blazing sun in near ecstasy. Nor did I have in mind encountering the elusive father in his crumpled linen jacket, his white skin reddened and freckled by the sun, whose remoteness had always, here in Spain, assumed the benign shape of the fisherman on the harbor wall, his blue beret less peculiar than at home, his feet in their rope-soled *alpargatas*, dangling above the oily water with unusual patience.

I sat down in that café where I would drink *café con leche* in the morning and cognac after dinner almost every day for the next three years. I didn't know I was trying to escape my startlingly dead parents by coming to the place where they had always been—and perhaps still might be—most alive. All I knew was that I needed to be here.

The Road to Perelada

I KNOW VERY LITTLE OF MY parents' life in Spain before I was born. They left so suddenly during the early weeks of the Civil War that they lost virtually all their possessions. I suppose that's why I never saw photographs of their friends, or of John and Ruth, who were seven and three when they hurried to the harbor and boarded one of the last ships out. Knowing so little, I took the trouble, some years ago, to search out the big, square house next to the old monastery in Pedralbes on the outskirts of Barcelona. It looked much the same as it must have when my parents lived there since that monastery and the cathedral were the only two churches in the city not damaged during the street fighting in '36. The house had been converted into apartments and remained mostly invisible behind its high stone wall, but I fancied I could see my mother pottering among the dense, perfumed shrubs and vines that I glimpsed through the wrought-iron gate, and I tried to conjure up my father, unimaginably young, as he swung that gate shut behind him and strode off with his sprinting walk down the hill to work.

The two of them had lived in Barcelona for much of their married life, but I never knew precisely why. My father's family, though English, lived in Cartagena, where they owned tin mines. My father and his brother had been sent off to English boarding schools, and then my father returned to Spain, though why he ended up working as an electrical engineer in Barcelona and not in the family mining business, I never thought to ask. Ours was not a family that encouraged curiosity about the past.

When my mother married my father, she married into a life abroad, which apparently agreed with her, as her love of Spain was fierce—so fierce, in fact, that for twenty-two years after the war she refused to return. At first it wasn't really a possibility, since they had little money and my father was trying to establish a business in London. Then there was World War II to endure, with heavy bombing along the south coast where they lived.

Soon after that, however, when the more immediate effects of the Civil War, but not the rubble of the second war, had been cleaned up, the British, eager to enjoy themselves after years of crisis and rationing, started to look south. My father wanted to join the crowds that were beginning to flock to the Costa Brava, but my mother held out: she knew it wouldn't be the same as when they had lived there. With angry glee she would produce as proof some picture in the travel section of the Sunday paper: Lloret de Mar, or, worse, Tossa, the tiny fishing village that had become a center for package tours, its shoddy hotels and fish-and-chip shops now catering to the British. I don't know what finally changed her mind. It might have been the fact that the King family, good friends of my parents in their Barcelona days, were planning a holiday in Caldetas. Or it might have been simply that my father's insistence wore her down, just as it must have done a few years later when she reluctantly agreed to go on that Christmas cruise.

CALDETAS was an unruly mixture of the old and the new, with the old giving up very little room to the new, which was why it suited my mother so well. She had come to know the town because many of the wives and children in the British colony before the war had spent their summers there, while the men worked in Barcelona and commuted out by train on the weekends. Built along a straight stretch of beach with no pretty coves like those that occur further north, Caldetas, I realized years later, reminded me of my hometown, Brighton. Both had a lively, rough-and-tumble center unconnected to the tourism that flowed around them. Both had areas of decaying grandeur, stately architecture, and wide esplanades where crowds of people strolled. If Jane Austen had written about Spain, it would have been Caldetas to which the flighty young woman ran away with her handsome officer, for both Caldetas and Brighton were watering places at heart.

It was hardly peaceful in Caldetas. The coastal highway intersected the town in such a way as to shake every building, as huge trucks trundled from France to Barcelona and points south. Trains, too, whistled through, following the straight line of the coast on rails that, outside the town, were dangerously unprotected. Every year a few unwary locals or tourists were killed as they hurried home from the beach or took a shortcut to the shops. In the town itself, each time a train came through, traffic on the maze of narrow streets would be halted, as railway crossing barriers descended with a din of warning bells that could be heard five miles west in the hills. Yet despite all this commotion, despite the sense of being built in the middle of a journey from somewhere to somewhere else, Caldetas retained a certain dignity—an untouched core of old-fashioned tranquillity.

Nowhere was this more apparent than at the Hotel Colón, a massive, off-white, Victorian structure with curved balustrades around its long terrace. If you walked up the semicircular steps from the esplanade on to the black and white tiles of the lobby, you found yourself moving back in time. Although it never, as far as I know, had an orchestra playing at tea time, it had the shady gentility, the reliable aspidistras, and the haughty staff that called for old violinists in moth-eaten morning coats. The usual clientele of businessmen and retired British and German couples was interspersed with very old, apparently very rich, regulars. There was the ninety-year-old *madrileña* who sat at her special table overlooking the beach, peering critically over her hooked nose at the label on a bottle of wine. And there were old men too, carrying polished canes, one even wearing spats.

It was 1957 and I was a lumpy thirteen-year-old that first time in the town we would return to summer after summer. We stayed at the Hotel Titus, a solidly respectable family hotel on the outskirts of town, where the mineral springs that had made Caldetas a spa town bubbled up and fed the sulphurous swimming pool, too warm for real swimming. I never spent much time on the premises but preferred to swim at the beach with a crowd of teenagers drawn from the Kings and other families.

The Kings were not actually all "Kings," but we thought of them that way. Germaine, for example, was named Barnett, a name she had acquired from a husband who was rarely mentioned and never seen. She operated a telephone switchboard for the Brazilian Embassy in London, where she plugged people in and out rapidly, chattering at full speed in five or six different languages. It was her older sister, Mona, who made the whole family regal by marrying a man twenty years her senior: Sir Norman King, the British Consul in Barcelona during the years my parents lived there. The children went by nicknames—Toto, Foufou, and Titi—which I found distinctly embarrassing, though none of the Kings seemed to find them unusual, not even later, when Toto soared up through the ranks of the British Navy and Germaine kept a photo of him in uniform in her tiny London flat, fondly captioned "Toto at his promotion to Lieutenant."

Those summer nights back in the fifties, my parents and I and all the Kings, joined by numerous Spanish friends, sat in an expanding circle at the little outdoor bar next to the bowling alley, my mother and Germaine drinking large quantities of Anis del Mono. Germaine's continental background had allowed her to escape my mother's thin layer of British good manners, and she always carried a small bottle of Anis in her handbag, from which she filled their glasses after they had bought two each from the bar. Mona, whose marriage to the British Consul endowed her with greater propriety, tut-tutted at her sister. In fact, the Kings were always hard up, and only managed these holidays by staying in cheap lodgings—a delightfully haphazard *pensión* next to the railway station, where they woke up each time the level crossing gates came down for a train.

It was the women in our party who laughed. Germaine and my mother wove fantasies into a zany humor that was unlike anything I had encountered in my proper British upbringing. My father, always quiet in social gatherings, sat next to Sir Norman and drank a beer or two, smiling benignly at the liveliness of our party, which often grew to twenty people. Those evenings would go on until two or three in the morning, the group talking animatedly in English, French, Spanish, and Catalan, the moon often brilliant above the dusty trees that divided the park from the railway.

Once in a while, Mona thought that the hilarity went too far and would gently reprove the guilty party. One night it was Germaine who was chastised (*"Qu'est-ce que tu fais, Germaine!*) after someone bet her she could not climb one of the ornate wrought-iron streetlights in the park. Aided and abetted by my tall mother, she swarmed up like a monkey.

Most nights we moved on from the bar to claim a spot at the bowling alley next door. There were six lanes, some of which were secured early each evening by means of bribes because they had fewer potholes in their cracked concrete—or, at least, potholes that skillful bowlers could avoid. The chipped wooden pins (which we called "skittles") stood on little round markers in the exact formation of modern American bowling alleys, but in the pit behind each set perched a small boy, chewing gum and swinging his legs until the ball came crashing down with the pins. Then he would throw his legs to one side or the other before climbing down to reset the pins and hurl the ball back down the wobbly, wooden conveyer. Every hour or two, a boy would get hit by a stray pin, sometimes just bruising a leg, but occasionally cracking him in the eye or head. If he had to be carried off to the *farmacia*, another would eagerly take his place.

The patrons of the alley were forever screaming at their *chicos*, who sometimes appeared not to notice that a ball had trundled into their domain, and at other times stood the pins back up in such disarray, so far off the little circular guides, that the customers would bellow and gesticulate, while the boy shrugged and grinned, as if to say, what can you do about it, eh?

These boys, most of whom were less than ten years old, were paid only in tips from the customers at the end of the evening. Any exasperated bowler who tried not tipping simply could not get a boy the next time he or she appeared. No amount of arguing with Domingo the bartender, who owned the alley, could produce a *chico* in the face of a boycott. There was solidarity among these workers.

Our party had no problems, however. Mona spent hours talking to the boys and knew all their names and most of their relatives' names too. My mother endeared herself by handing out sherbert lemons and by continuing to bowl every evening despite her inability to hit even one pin. When we arrived at the park, a dozen or more children would run up to us begging to be "our boy" for the evening, clowning for the privilege. Three or four would run backwards in front of my mother, shading their eyes with one hand and looking up with awe. *"¡Qué alta! ¡Qué alta!"* they would say with mock reverence, as if my mother's statuesque presence somehow approached sainthood.

Germaine chattered in a constant stream of English, French,

and Spanish, waving her arms and lifting her pencilled eyebrows comically. Occasionally she paused to pull out her lipstick and a little green compact, pursed her lips into a pouty kiss, and renewed the scarlet lips that made her look like a movie star of the forties. Both she and Mona were under five feet tall and had short, very flat, fair hair that gave them an elfin appearance, especially when seen from a distance, walking arm in arm as if they might burst into a synchronized dance at any moment. My mother, with her wiry grey hair, her feet that bulged out of her shoes, and her big, laughing face, always looked ungainly beside the two of them. But when she and Germaine got going, spinning out some exaggerated version of an adventure they had had, or making up scandalous tales about people we saw at the bar, my mother's eloquence transcended her physical awkwardness. When she threw her head back and laughed, she grew elegant.

In fact, that summer when I was thirteen, my mother in her new relaxed form was a different person than the one I had always known. When she spoke Spanish, her hands and arms swooped and circled as if they had escaped the chains of her English life and, for the first time, I began to glimpse her anguish at leaving this balmy Mediterranean atmosphere.

Thinking about those vacations now, I can barely capture their essence—the ingredient that made us such a charmed group—but I know that everyone who was there looked back on those summers in Caldetas with a nostalgia that has lingered through the years, obliterating the squabbles that must have erupted and the secrets that surely hovered in the shadows around our spotlight. For a few years, we mythologized ourselves in a year-round correspondence that began when I created a spoof newspaper. Front-page articles described the carryings-on of a strange "sect," observed, of course, in Caldetas, and right in the center of the patched-together page, I placed a photograph of myself as "Queen of Bowling," holding a ball aloft—a triumph of cut-and-paste, which provoked a spate of admiring correspondence and a rival "newspaper clipping" from the Kings.

These reports, of course, left a lot out. Like the summer I turned sixteen, when I barely saw my family or friends and pursued instead a number of torrid romances, ranging from chaste and proper dates with Toto to illicit encounters under the pines with Thierry, a Frenchman who seemed very old. He was perhaps thirty or forty—I wouldn't have known the difference—and was intent on getting his head up my very tight, straight skirt, while I wondered what he so badly wanted to look at. Night after night I staggered back to the Titus, often quite drunk, to be greeted by the night porter exposing himself from baggy blue pants and threatening to tell my parents what time I had returned if I didn't stay and look at his eagerly erect penis.

Occasionally, Germaine and Foufou came to visit us in Brighton. My mother and Germaine immediately reverted to their Caldetas selves and my father grew gloomy with disapproval, as dinners in the kitchen were punctuated by loud songs, the two of them singing nonsense and banging on a variety of pots and pans, while Foufou and I accompanied them on the recorder and kazoo. When the four of us broke out a bottle of duty-free Anis del Mono and started dancing in a circle to our one precious record of *sardanas*, my father took his library book and shut himself in the bedroom.

Still, these Brighton antics were only a rehearsal for the real thing, which would always take place on balmy evenings by the Mediterranean—evenings like the one when six or seven of us decided to go swimming. Plunging into the water in a burst of green fire, we trailed a wake of phosphorescence as we paddled around under the stars. *"Formidable!"* Germaine trilled, thrilling me with her ability to articulate so perfectly the magic of the moment. *"Vraiment formidable!"*

Later that night my mother and I walked back alone to the Hotel Titus, past the grand old villas that stood back from the esplanade behind high walls and intricate, wrought-iron gates. As we passed one of these houses at two in the morning, the sound of music drifted out: a song that was popular that year called "Green Fields." It's easy, even today, to evoke that melancholy tune and see the mansion with its pungent oleanders, its vine-covered terrace, its old blue tiles surrounding archways and patios. That night, my mother's sadness about leaving Spain seemed almost to form itself into words, but she held back from explanation and stood instead for a long time outside the gates, looking across the coarse, manicured grass, while the music hauntingly insinuated itself into my memory.

THE Hotel Paris, where my Perelada employers put me up in 1964, was right on the central square of Figueras, a sprawling little market town just off the main highway from Perpignan to Barcelona. Every Thursday, vendors and shoppers from all over the region invaded the town, which accounted for its disproportionate number of restaurants and stores. The square, always referred to as the *rambla*, was a long, rectangular patch of concrete, raised three steps' height from the sidewalks that surrounded it, and shaded on all sides by tall trees. Ornate iron benches, covered with layers of bird shit that only disappeared after a rainstorm, surrounded the open area, where hundreds of people strolled up and down before dinner. Old people sat on the benches chattering even more loudly than the birds that clustered in the branches above, fighting for the best roosting spots. Small children, dressed in ruffled shirts or dresses and shiny patent leather shoes, dashed among the strollers' legs or jumped rope in front of doting grandmothers.

Traffic rushed along the road that surrounded the *rambla*, while on two sides of the outer perimeter, cafés sprawled across broad sidewalks, the red and white checked tablecloths of one establishment giving way to the varnished wooden tabletops of the next. Waiters, immaculate in their black and white, greeted each passerby with resignation, knowing only too well that people rarely abandoned their regular spots. Tourists, however, brought them to life and they would bow and smile their invitations at the French and English families who stopped off on their way to the coast.

The Hotel Paris was nestled in among these cafés, its dining room on the second floor looking out on to the *rambla*, while my room, on the fourth floor at the back, looked down on one of the narrow streets that led to the market square just a couple of blocks away. Opposite my window, with its miniature balcony and iron grille, a whole block of similar balconies displayed geraniums, washing lines, and a variety of wooden shutters, some with peeling grey paint, others newly green. The old woman across the way always shook her finger at me and winked after the time my almost-dry underwear blew off my balcony and ended up being presented by her grandchildren to Señor Fernando, the hotel manager, who carried his circular paunch in front of him as a mallard duck carries his gleaming green breast.

From Figueras, it was a ten-minute drive to Perelada. There, the centuries-old houses covered a perfectly conical hill that rose out of the flat Ampurdán plain and was crowned by the church. Approaching the village, the narrow road wound between walls of corn, and the distant Pyrenees fell in a backdrop of craggy steps from their grandiose, indigo heights to the ocean. Perelada stood up from the plain like a cardboard cutout. The fields were fertile, producing crops and animals that ended up at the weekly market in Figueras, and, on the lower slopes that rose from the plain, miles of cooperatively owned vineyards produced the fruit that fueled Perelada's industry. Once you left the flats, however, and climbed into the higher land between the plain and rugged coastline, farms and vineyards gave way to rolling hills dotted with sage and occasional cork or olive trees. It was a landscape of tortoises and prickly pears, alive with crickets and crisscrossed with arroyos. I quickly grew to love the wrinkled rocks, the smell of the hot earth, and the heat that drifted up from the ground, as if someone in the underworld were always cooking.

Life quickly acquired a certain routine that not only took me back and forth between Figueras and Perelada but also along the straight, potholed road from Figueras, or over the snaky road from Perelada, to the beach resort of Rosas, and sometimes on from there over the mountain of Cabo Creus to the alleys and coves of Cadaqués. I danced at discos, drank like a trooper, drove my car through the night at ninety, and had unrewarding sex with virtual strangers on the beach, watching out for the *guardias* who patrolled to limit such activity.

Sometimes a love-struck waiter I had picked up at a disco or a hopeful student I had chatted with over a brandy would show up in Figueras. They would come to my hotel, where Señor Fernando gravely asked their names and sent a maid to fetch me if I was up in my room. This diminutive, fatherly man once ventured to warn me about one of these admirers, telling me in a confidential voice that he was a *no buen chico*. I probably knew this already, but I wasn't interested in good boys. I thanked him for his warning and told the not-good-boy to go away, which is probably what I would have done anyway, since I didn't like my night life intruding into my day life.

In Figueras, I knew only Spaniards—though they would have hated me to call them that, since Catalan nationalism, viciously suppressed by Franco, was nevertheless cautiously rampant. I hung out with the young Catalan men at a café in the *rambla*, and had friends and acquaintances all over town, from Emilia in her dusty store with its sacks spilling out lentils and chick peas, to Salvador, the head waiter at the fancy Hotel Durán. I shopped in the market, discussed the weather with the old men who sat all day at the Café Luna, and had my car, my hair, and my sandals fixed by neighbors. I was the only foreigner living in town, and I worked very hard at fitting in.

People were so different here. Women, for example, screamed at the top of their lungs if they were moved to do so. They screamed at children, at men, at shopkeepers who wouldn't sell olive oil or garbanzos at the right price. Sometimes they screamed in anger; sometimes in joy. They got a little quieter when they expressed their love, which was perhaps no more abundant than the British love I had grown up with, but a lot more accessible. You knew not only that they had feelings, but what those feelings were at any given moment. In England, feelings had not been public information, and until I lived in Spain it didn't occur to me that they could be.

"*¡Ay, pobrecita!*" exclaimed Rosa, my hairdresser, when she discovered my parents had died six months earlier. Her eyes filled with tears as she enveloped me in a hug from behind, prickly rollers in each hand, comb and scissors falling to the floor. She looked up into the mirror and saw my embarrassed face. I wasn't crying, which was clearly what she expected me to do. It wasn't that I immediately learned demonstrative behavior from my new friends—in fact, I remained as unable to gain access to my own emotions as ever—but I was satisfied, even comforted, by their willingness to do it on my behalf.

It was the combination of being welcomed and liked, and being able to imagine myself part of this culture, that gave every moment in Figueras a clarity that I felt each morning as I stepped out of the cool, shady lobby of the Hotel Paris on to the sidewalk in front of the *rambla*. Just before I turned right to my usual table, my *café con leche*, and a hunk of chewy bread, the intense weight of the early morning heat would envelop my body. As the heat entered the pores of my skin, I felt myself absorb everything else too: the particular notes of the car engines, different from the engines of Fords or Austins; the unmistakable vowels and consonants in the shouts of people greeting each other; the unique rustle of the leaves high overhead as the sycamores swayed in a slight breeze; and the intense blue of the sky behind the green that belonged only to those leaves.

Taking that first step down from the marbled hotel entrance, I felt the full force of my displacement, even while I sank completely into the life I had chosen. The coffee steamed in its thick white cup, frothy and fragrant with that unique combination of bitter and sweet created by the flavor of good coffee and Spanish milk. The bread was dusted with flour on its hard crust. I bit into it as if I had known it through all the centuries it had been made in this town, while at the very same time, I noted its taste in that special way one notices only what is new and different.

One day, the daughter of a close friend of my mother's turned up unexpectedly. Heather was a flamboyant character with wild auburn hair and a fluent command of Spanish, which she spoke with a sibilant Argentine accent. She had somehow finagled an invitation to stay at Salvador Dalí's house in Port Lligat. Dalí, the brilliantly subversive leader of the surrealist movement who later became something of a money-making exhibitionist, was in the sixties a kind of father-figure to the flower children of Europe and America. He had been leading a very public, hedonistic life for at least three decades on the beach, just north of Cadaqués.

Heather persuaded me to deliver her to Port Lligat and made me promise to pick her up a few days later and drive her to Perpignan Airport. Not assertive enough to extract even an introduction to the great man in return for my services, I did as she asked, picking her up on the appointed day to discover that she was returning to England with a five-foot statue in tow. It barely fit into the back of my open car, but I managed to get the two of them to the airport, only to find that Heather needed a substantial loan to pay for the statue's transportation. Rueful at my gullibility, I paid the bill and drove back to Figueras from the airport feeling suddenly quite bereft.

Later that night, sitting at the café with the group of young men who had become my friends, I told them the story, sparing Heather none of the mockery I had learned to heap on foolish foreigners. As we laughed together, my sense of abandonment gradually dispersed. The *rambla* warmed me with its now-familiar sounds of trucks and scraping chairs, its comforting smells of exhaust and eau de cologne, and I forgot about that other world—the one where Heather was probably at this very minute recounting her Dalíesque adventures to her intellectual London crowd, or perhaps even talking on the phone to her mother. Her mother, who had been a friend of my mother's.

"Ay, qué chica tan rara!" I said, firmly severing my connection to Heather and sinking, once again, into the illusion of belonging. The boys were still chuckling about her as I ordered another cognac and looked up at the stars bobbing across the sky like ships' lights on an ocean. The cognac came and, lifting the small bubble of a glass to my lips, I felt the amber liquid spill across my tongue, seep into all the pockets of my mouth, and run down my throat till it burned like a secret in the pit of my stomach. I looked around the table at the faces of these new friends—these strangers who knew nothing about me except what I was creating minute by minute.

The Initiation

JOSÉ MARÍA ALBERNY WAS the son of the butcher. He was older than the gang he hung out with—the band of young men of which I had become an honorary member. I didn't exactly become "one of the boys"; I was always obviously different. Though most of them were about my age or a couple of years older, how could I fail to be different at six feet tall, towering over all of them except Alberny, who was my height if I took off my shoes? And there was my blond hair, the fine, silky hair I had inherited from my father (though I had to work hard to remove the curls that came from my mother), now bleached almost white by salt and sun. The boys were all so dark with their olive skin and black hair—all, that is, except for Jaime, whose medium brown hair and bluish eyes won him the nickname of Jaime El Rubio, though in most company from the northern climes he would have been just a nondescript darkish-haired boy.

No, I was hardly one of the boys, although I was admitted to the group as no other female was. Spanish girls didn't get to go out alone, much less sit in cafés after dinner drinking coffee and cognac. They couldn't pile into someone's car, heading for one of the local village fiestas. Spanish girls appeared together in groups, walking arm in arm up and down the *rambla* before dinner. One or two of them were engaged to boys in Alberny's gang, but I never saw the happy couples together. As for foreign girls, they were simply prey, especially the blondes: legitimate targets, the boys thought, for their macho exhibitionism. Somehow my proximity—my appearance in the café at breakfast time and after dinner, my frequent shopping trips at the weekly market, and my regular appointments with Alberny's aunt-by-marriage, the hairdresser on Calle Gerona— put me outside the category of legitimate prey. To pursue foreign girls required a trip to the artificial world of beach resorts and nightclubs, a trip far away from this very traditional world. I was too close to home, almost family, or at least an honorary townsgirl, a girl whose reputation needed protection, even though I myself clearly showed no respect for proper behavior. Night after night, I scandalized the population of Figueras by roaring back from the beach at three or four in the morning in my little sports car. But day after day, I lived among them, shopping and gossiping like anybody else, and, perhaps because I didn't act guilty or evasive about the nocturnal adventures, they rallied around me as they would have rallied around a wayward daughter of the town. In fact, looking back on it now, I think they were, in some mysterious way, proud of my independence—proud to allow me, by virtue of my foreignness, the freedom none of them could claim.

I spent most of my time with all the boys together. Isidro's father would sometimes lend us his taxi for a group outing, while three or four more could pile into my little open Triumph, with a couple sitting up precariously on the back. This was how we traveled to the fiesta at San Pablo de la Roca—my first fiesta. As we bumped into the village over cobbles liberally sprinkled with mule dung, my passengers lurched and shouted with excitement. The crisp roar of our exhaust echoed between the ancient walls of the convent and the old town fortifications, as people jumped aside shouting ¡caramba! and whistling at our festive appearance. Over the next three hours, I won a purple rabbit for shooting a hole in a plastic egg, danced three *sardanas,* towering over the circle of precise dancers, barely escaped throwing up in the swingboats, and was stared at long and hard by everybody in the crowd (to which I was perfectly accustomed by this time).

At Bañolas lake, where the world water-skiing championships were being held, we all lounged in the shade of weeping willow trees eating *tortillas españolas* pressed between hunks of fresh bread, while the speedboats roared up and down the lake, and the skiers, like Canadian geese in early fall, swooped hither and thither and, once in a while, plunged clumsily into the water with ill-timed excitement. As the afternoon turned to dusk, we clowned in front of someone's camera, producing a few overexposed snapshots that I still have somewhere in the bottom of a drawer.

There were times, however, when I would abandon the group and go out on a date with one or other of the boys. Jaime

El Rubio took me to Granny's Nightclub in Rosas; Isidro took me to dinner at the Camping Pous, where he taught me to drink from a *purrón* and I poured red wine down the front of my dress; and José Vasquez took me to a dinner dance at the luxurious Hotel Cap Sa Sal at Aiguablava, where they later filmed a James Bond movie. Looking back on it, I wonder how much these dates had to do with the Triumph, which all the boys worshiped unreservedly, and how much with me. Anyway, regardless of the car appeal, I suspect the group had an agreement about me—maybe one that Alberny had created and enforced. In marked contrast to virtually every other date during my three years in Spain, none of the gang ever tried anything sexual with me. They very properly escorted me home to my door and shook my hand, or once in a while offered a chaste kiss on the cheek. Again I was getting treated like a girl who lived among them might be treated—though of course she might never be allowed to go on the date in the first place.

The two dates I had with Alberny himself were different. While the other boys acted as if I were someone's cousin visiting from Palafrugell, who should be given a good time but treated as family, Alberny, having instigated this policy, clearly had the option of abandoning it if he chose—and sometimes he seemed close to doing so. His power fascinated me. It was probably what made him the only one in the group I found attractive. I have sometimes wondered if I acted seductive when we were alone, but that time is hard to conjure up, perhaps because I had no self-awareness, no ability to analyze what was happening. I lived from day to day, recording in my small diary only the bare facts: *Went to Cap Sa Sal with J.M. Danced till 2.* Or *Drinks with the gang. Alberny left early.*

I certainly felt intensely intimate with Alberny that day we watched the sunset from the highest hill in the park outside town, sitting on a bed of aromatic pine needles, the light melting away into a solid black wall of cicada song. I might well have been afraid, even angry, if he had succeeded in putting aside his obvious conflict and grabbed me, but the truth was I liked his moody, foreboding silences, during which I deduced, as perhaps he meant me to, that he was virtuously grappling with an overwhelming desire to kiss me. I liked his "big brother" protective stance, mixed with the dangerous possibilities of his too-intense gaze. I liked his slicked-back hair and his black jeans and his attention.

Alberny was uneducated, arrogant, and full of the prejudices common to Catalans at that time but, even after what happened later, I couldn't write him off as a mean person. He had excessive amounts of certain Spanish male traits—a reverence for his mother and mothers in general, an impatient desire to have children, and an intense pride in who he was and in his people. "His people" included family, all the townsfolk (except *guardias* and those shadowy figures who had become rich by throwing in their lot with Franco), and all Catalans. They also included the English, the Dutch, and the Americans, many of whom he went out of his way to meet as they passed through Figueras, setting himself up as a kind of host and town guide, though he spoke no English. He would lead whole families to the café, sit down with them and order them San Miguel beers or cognacs, which he would refuse to let them pay for. When they remonstrated, he would wave his hand graciously and tell them in Catalan that such a thing was unthinkable. "His people," however, did not stretch to include the Italians, the Germans, the French, or Spaniards from Andalusia, these last of whom he considered an embarrassment to the country because of their poverty, their short stature, and their "uneducated" speech. Perhaps it was Alberny's pride, or some mysterious aspect of his machismo, that led to what happened that Thursday night in August, though I'm not at all sure about his motivation, and even less sure about my own.

We were all sitting outside the café—perhaps ten of us at a table right next to the curb. Trucks rattled past, blowing out billows of noxious fumes and drowning out pieces of the conversation. It was about ten in the evening and our group was still expanding as the boys wandered out from their mothers' dinner tables. I sat next to Alberny, who dominated the group with his particular intensity and by virtue of being the oldest. Jaime El Rubio was there. So was Francisco, who worked at the *farmacia*. Isidro sat silent behind his round wire-rim glasses, which had led me to mistake him for an intellectual when I first saw him. Blanc, with his lock of black hair falling over his forehead, smiled and offered me cigarettes. They all talked very fast in Catalan but whenever anyone addressed me directly, he switched to Castilian. My presence and their good manners, however, could not hold them to a language less familiar, and certainly less beloved, than the one they grew up with.

Soon the conversation started to revolve around me: my independence; my ability to live alone, travel alone, drive a fast car, stay out dancing until dawn, and generally do whatever I wanted without consulting anyone. The boys were not deterred by my embarrassment. "She's tough," someone said, with admiration. "Yes, tough like a boy," agreed someone else. But Alberny demurred. "She's a girl," he said flatly. "No girl is tough like a boy," and his dark eyes turned to me with a challenge.

There was a moment's silence. Though I certainly didn't think about it at the time, I now see that I was meant to agree: to giggle like a girl, maybe to argue ineffectively and defer to his masculinity. I suppose this was just one of several openings he created through which I could have embarked upon a spectacular but doomed affair. But I never saw the possibility—at least, not on those terms. I didn't have it in me to giggle and assent to the assumption of my feminine weakness.

"She's tough, is she?" Alberny said mockingly, his eyes never leaving mine as he scraped his chair up close and took a drag of his black-tobacco cigarette, leaving it between his lips while the strong-smelling smoke wound up in front of his eyes and around his greased-back cowlick. "I don't think she's so very tough, you know." And he smiled at me, at first gently, and then with the full force of his charm and male arrogance.

Still I remained silent. Slowly he brought up his hand and removed the cigarette. Slowly he lowered his hand with the cigarette between his thumb and forefinger till he was holding it, glowing tip down, a few inches above the back of my right hand, which was resting on the white iron table. "No," he said, still smiling. "She doesn't like to get hurt. She's just like all the girls."

This was another opening for me. I could still giggle and defer, but again I did not understand. These rituals had somehow escaped my education and, to this day, I can't explain why. Most of my friends had learned how to play this game with boys, but I had always stubbornly, and painfully, held back. So instead of grabbing his wrist and laughingly agreeing with him—instead of a coy *Oh, José María, of course I don't like to get hurt!*, I simply stared back at him. I dare say there was as much challenge in my stare as in his, as our gazes interlocked like the interlocking of two arm wrestlers' hands. It was a decisive moment. The joke evaporated and something serious was afoot.

All the boys fell silent. The traffic kept up its din, but our table sat as if in its own protected bubble of quietness. Antonio, the waiter, stopped clearing a nearby table and froze, his tray held high, as Alberny's cigarette came closer and closer to the back of my hand. Alberny's fingers were shaking very slightly and the dark smoke continued to spiral its way up into the large sunshade that covered the table, gathering in a murky pocket under the words Martini Blanco, that showed red through the white canvas. Then I could feel the warmth approach my skin. Alberny's eyes seemed to flash. His mouth curved a little as he waited for me to jerk back my hand and jump up. The joke could still work and he believed it would. But still I stared into his eyes. I saw him hesitate. I saw his eyes glance quickly towards my hand, checking out how close the glowing cigarette was to my tanned skin. And then I saw his inability to back down.

Alberny set his lips in a grim expression that would probably become a permanent part of his middle-aged face, and moved the cigarette down. I never moved. Never flinched—not at the first touch and not as the pain set in. There was a smell of burning flesh and there were tears in my eyes, but they did not overflow and I did not move a muscle as I continued to stare into Alberny's eyes. After what seemed like a very long time—but might actually have been five or ten seconds—he looked down at my hand, removed the cigarette and tossed it into the street. "Wait here," he said in a matter-of-fact tone, "I'll get you something for it." As he walked away from the café, his shoulders drooped just a little.

The boys started talking again. Blanc put an arm around my shoulder and asked if I was okay, while Antonio started to clatter his cups and spoons. I nodded and breathed—then breathed some more, concentrating on not feeling anything beyond the intense pain on my right hand, until Alberny returned with antiseptic ointment and bandaids. Very gently he dressed the small round wound, which was quite deep and throbbing now. When he was done, he smiled at me—a smile of complicity with no challenge left in it—and ordered a brandy for me. Maybe it was then, or maybe a day or so later, when I continued to appear with the wound covered, that he said, "So, I've made my mark on you, haven't I?"

I don't remember anything else about that night: how I left or at what time. Nor do I recall how long the burn took to heal. All I know is that Alberny treated me differently after that. I might have been his sister—not a little sister, but one the same age as him or older. He was still protective, but now there was unambiguous respect. His conflict was gone, the door to passion closed forever: our relationship and something important about the rest of my life both decided.

Paco's Mother

DOLORES WAS ONE OF THOSE large-boned Catalans, taller than most Spanish women; taller than many of the men in the village of Perelada. Almost as tall as me, in fact. Certainly as tall as my mother had been, and about the same build. I knew from the way she walked slowly home on her large legs with the knotted veins showing through thick stockings that she was actually less sturdy than the smaller women who chattered energetically beside her all day at work. My mother had been like that too.

Her son, Paco, was at least a head taller but half as wide. His arm bones stretched out much finer than his mother's and his wrists protruded far beyond the cuffs of his grey shirt. His blue workman's trousers flapped loose and short on his legs and, although in 1964 he was only twenty-seven, already he had a pronounced stoop from leaning down to talk with his smaller companions, and a prematurely balding head, which made him look close to forty. When I started as tour guide, Dolores worked on the bottling and labeling line at Las Cavas, and Paco was the foreman in charge of delivery trucks. Each of them, like 99 percent of the villagers, played a small part in the production of Perelada wines and champagnes.

Dolores was the third in a line of twelve women who sometimes slapped the labels on to the green champagne bottles that wobbled along a metal conveyor belt and sometimes wiped the dust off the bottles that trundled up through the trapdoor from the cellars. As I went about my business in and around the bottling plant, my eyes followed her broad hands, picking up labels one after another and, later in the afternoon, her tired back as it disappeared up the hill towards her house near the church. A certain movement here, an awkwardness there, sparked a kind of recognition—a strange feeling of familiarity I never stopped to examine. Somewhere just under my brittle surface, I cherished a desire to feel her arms around me, to rest my head on her competent, comforting breast.

I learned, from gossiping with Rosé and María, who ran the bar, that Dolores had worked on the line for thirty-eight years, starting on her sixteenth birthday. No one had expected her to marry: she was too tall. But in 1935, long after everyone, herself included, had given up bemoaning her ill fortune, Salvador the butcher had taken her to the altar and she had left the sisterhood of the bottling line for Salvador's meat shop on Calle Gerona. There she plucked scrawny chickens while screaming her contributions to the news of the day with her customers.

"Oígame, señora," she would bellow above the raucous chatter in the dark shop. "I've got the strangest thing to tell you!" Only she did not speak in the melodious Castilian Spanish which sweeps up on its penultimate syllables and gracefully slides away on its final O's or A's. Instead she used the high-pitched, nasal Catalan, which chops off its endings and seals them shut with percussive T's, as finite as the axe strokes that sliced through Dolores's chicken necks onto the scarred chopping block.

Her time out from the bottling line lasted just three years. Salvador was killed fighting up in the hills during the second year of the Civil War and the butcher's shop passed to his brother. Dolores, who didn't want to run the business alone, was glad to rejoin the sisterhood and soon it was as if she had never left. Paco was too young to remember his father, and Dolores forgot him too, once a respectful period of mourning had been observed. From then on she wore only black.

The women welcomed her back, and, like women the world over in times of war, they kept things running smoothly and even prided themselves on making some improvements. But now in 1964 the men were securely back in charge, and the office had expanded into a new concrete building, where several bureaucrats with rolled-up shirtsleeves and green shades on their foreheads, sat at desks behind stacks of papers, which they scrutinized, wrote on, and stamped with an array of rubber stamps. There was a wine-tasting bar on the road through the village, with tables outside and a free glass of champagne for everyone who toured the wine cellars. A fleet of container trucks and delivery vans came and went from the loading bays behind the garden, supervised by Paco, who leaned against one door post or another with a sheaf of documents in his hand, running his other hand over his bald head. Sometimes, when I had stayed up particularly late in some nightclub or other, I would back my car into the garden during the quiet afternoon and, shaded by the overhead vine, sleep off my exhaustion for an hour or two. Paco, I later found out, covered for me when he saw my green Triumph out there among the dusty oleanders.

On grey days, when the tourists didn't want to sit on dull beaches, busloads would pull up beside the Perelada bar, opposite the castle wall. As they tumbled out, sunburned and clumsy, Paco and the idle truck drivers would watch them amble up the driveway to the office, and make bets on their nationality.

"Hay trabajo, Judith," one of my office mates would say, pointing through the window to the big tour bus parked in the lot beside my car. When referring to my work, the clerks' voices never quite lost the mocking tone they had acquired during my first few weeks, when I actually did no work at all, but spent my days in the castle, learning about its history from Martín, the librarian, so I could conduct reasonably intelligent tours. Although I rushed around quite busily now, teaching large groups how champagne is made and recounting how the first Count of Perelada once entered the chapel on his horse in full armor, most of the workers treated me as if what I did was not real work.

Sometimes, if I was lounging around with the drivers, I would set them straight about their bets. "No, no, no!" I would exclaim in mock horror. "They can't be Italians—no Italian would be seen dead in that polyester. And look at the colors! *¡Qué horror!"* Paco was always relieved to learn they were not Italians, since a group from Milano had once left with champagne bottles tucked into their jackets and beach bags. Paco thought that the English and the Dutch, unlike the Italians, were scrupulously honest, and he approved of them in spite of their terrible habit of wearing socks with their sandals.

There weren't many Americans, of course, but when an occasional family came through in a rented car, everyone in Las Cavas perked up. Large tips had been known to find their way into Paco's hand for no particular reason, and even the women on the line had once picked up a hundred-peseta bill. As for me, I knew a thousand was coming my way at the end of my guided tour, and after a liberal tasting at the bar. Americans always left with several cases of the special reserve in the trunks of their cars, and sometimes, in the afterglow of *semisec* or brut, they invited me to some rented villa at Llansá or Ampurias for water skiing and barbecue.

On busy afternoons, I walked up and down the drive between the cellars and the bar many times, sometimes at the head of a straggly busload, sometimes in intimate conversation with a carload. Paco lolled against his door post and followed me with his eyes. Later I would return, sleepily relaxed from all the champagne I had shared with the clients, and wander through the plant, where I, in turn, followed Dolores with my eyes as she deftly placed label after label in exactly the right place, moving in a rhythm that bore no relation to the rhythms of her constant talk.

I had never said anything to her beyond a general *buenos días* and an occasional exclamation about last night's weather or, on one occasion, the floods that swept several cars out to sea at Ampurias. "*¡Ay!*" she volunteered in that particular conversation, smiling at me rather unexpectedly: "It's dangerous to park in the river beds. What do they expect...?" And it was

69

only out of deference to me that she bit her tongue on the logical end to her remark: "...those foreigners!"

One day she beckoned to me conspiratorially with her forefinger during a break. She was by herself in a dark part of the factory, looking around to make sure that no one noticed. "Psssst, *señorita*. Pssst, *señorita*," she hissed, until I hurried over. She grasped my arm and led me round the back of the three huge fermenting vats next to the laboratory. Then she let out a stream of Catalan, smiling excessively at me between phrases, but I could not follow her. "*Lentamente*," I begged, so she switched to the formal Spanish that almost everyone used with me.

"Please come and visit my home," she said. And with a smile that seemed particularly ingratiating: "My son would like it very much too. Come for a glass of sherry after work on Friday." Since everyone drank Perelada wine all the time, and Perelada did not produce sherry, and since I had never been invited to anyone's home before, I deduced that this must be a special occasion.

On the appointed day, I left my car at the bar and set off on foot along the cobbled streets that were too narrow for cars but wide enough for the donkey carts that trundled around, hauling building materials, orange butane canisters, or sacks of potatoes. I climbed a little and then traversed the slope until I came to Calle San Antonio. Like all the other streets, it was lined with rows of centuries-old, whitish houses, ten or twelve joined together in a terrace, with red-tiled flat roofs. Lines of washing blew in the breeze along the rooftops and music blared out of the upstairs windows, which had little iron grilles in front of them. All the ground floor doors were thick and wooden, split into two. The bottom halves were mostly closed;

the tops open. I peered over some of them into the dark, smelly interiors, where a couple of goats or some rangy brown sheep would be munching or dozing.

Number 62 was no different. The downstairs door stood wide open and there were no animals inside, although a bed of clean straw awaited some resident's return. I entered cautiously, my eyes slowly adapting to the stable, which had no windows and a lot of cobwebs, until I saw the staircase that went up one wall. Should I knock on the outside door? No one would hear if I did. I opted for the staircase, and for calling out "¿Señora? ¿Señora?" as I approached the archway at the top that led into the human part of the house.

Dolores bustled to meet me, wearing a black dress I had never seen before made of some kind of shiny material, and a lace shawl around her shoulders. She had a dab of lipstick on too. "Paco, Paco," she called through another archway into a room where a TV set murmured. Paco appeared, also looking unlike himself in black creased pants and a white shirt. He stuck out his hand sheepishly and muttered, "mucho gusto."

Sweet sherry was served in tiny green glasses that looked as if they were made from the same glass as the champagne and wine bottles. On the table was a basket of sticky cakes, some filled with cream, others shedding powdered sugar. Plastic flowers in little hanging pots decorated the stucco walls, between a crucifix and plates that displayed the Catalan flag or said *Recuerdo de Cadaqués*.

Conversation proved extremely difficult. I balanced a powdery cake on a napkin, sipped my sherry, and asked Dolores if she had any other children, which she didn't. Paco wanted to know about England, but I had difficulty with both his and my own language. Or was it more than just language? How could I describe England to these people, neither of whom had ever even been to Barcelona? They had seen magazine pictures of the Queen on her official birthday, riding Winston, whose name they remembered because Paco smoked Winston cigarettes, and they seemed to think that everyone lived like royalty there. Dolores asked about my family, and when I told her my parents were dead, her eyes filled with tears. "*¡Qué desgracia!*" she murmured, reaching out to hold my arm for a moment. Somewhere beneath consciousness, I felt enveloped in her embrace, as I repressed all knowledge of the tears that lay behind my careful smile. Then she flung a string of questions at me about how my parents had managed to die while I was still so young.

As the conversation wound down, Paco, who had hardly spoken, excused himself and wandered off downstairs. After a brief silence, Dolores asked: "Do you have a *novio?*" This was not new to me, since every Spaniard I had met found a way to ask me within the first ten minutes if I had a boyfriend or fiancé. Usually when faced with the question, I just laughed and said no, pushing down my discomfort at the universal assumption that I ought to be preparing to get married. This was something else I was working hard not to think about. Perhaps I knew that if I thought about it, I might have to speculate, not only about marriage but also about heterosexuality. Such speculation was unthinkable in this Spanish world of the early sixties and in my own state of unacknowledged fragility.

But Dolores' question, "*¿Tiene usted novio?*" seemed particularly weighted. It was the question I had been invited to her house to answer. "No," I said, trying to laugh it off as usual. But she persisted. "Paco would make a good husband," she volunteered. "He's a good worker. He's already been promoted to foreman, and Señor Dominguez says he'll go higher in time." She scrutinized my face, which was probably registering shock, as I checked out if I was understanding her properly. Then she played her trump card. "And he's very tall." Again she paused. Still I didn't react. "Taller than you," she urged, not pointing out how few men were taller than I. But the unspoken words hung in the air. Surely I would snap up the first one over six feet who was willing.

I tried to get out of the house with good grace. I said thank you; I had to go; had an appointment; would think about Paco. I agreed he was a good boy; a hard worker like her. I flattered her and then I fled down the hollowed-out stairs and burst into the street.

As I walked back to the bar to pick up my car and drive to Figueras, I realized that this had been something large in the lives of Dolores and Paco—that he must have enlisted her help, since she never would have thought of me as a possible daughter-in-law on her own. Or would she? Could she have picked up on my yearning for the mother I had lost, whom she so oddly resembled? Anyway, no matter how it had started, it was serious now. I imagined Paco rushing back to the house when he saw my car was gone. I imagined his eagerness. "What did she say, Mamá?"

I never even remotely considered pursuing Paco. The chasm between us was vaster than I could comprehend or articulate. I was playing at life in Perelada but had no concept at all of what it would be like to take on for real. Being an outsider was temporary—a distraction from grief; the possibility of becoming an insider, unimaginable.

For a few weeks Paco blushed a deep red whenever I passed

him at Las Cavas. I would give him a cheery hello, and he would mutter. Dolores never invited me back to her home, and no one else in the village did either. Home invitations, I gradually learned, were for family, very close family friends, or potential family only. But she seemed to bear me no grudge for my unwillingness to join her tall family, and I, in turn, held on to a special fondness for her that would prove only the first in a series of attachments to the mothers of eligible sons, all of whom failed to realize that I was more interested in a mother-in-law than a husband.

For months I continued to smile warmly at Dolores and engage her in conversation if I could, until one day, in the midst of a chat about the weather, I put my hand on hers and said, apropos of nothing: "Dolores, I really don't think I'll get married for a long time."

She patted my hand as if she had been waiting for this. "*Ay, ay,*" she sighed, sadly resigned to the odd ways of modern and very foreign young women. "I thought that might be the case." Then she looked me right in the eyes with a great sadness—perhaps for the romance that was not to be—perhaps for my own premature orphanhood. "*¡Qué lástima!*" she said, as I felt, once again, that desire to throw myself into her arms. "What a pity!"

Señor Serra's Romance

I NEVER KNEW HIS FIRST NAME: Señor Serra was what I always called him. Over evening coffees and cognacs in one or other of the cafés that surrounded the *rambla*, I met a large proportion of the male population, but Señor Serra was the one I most liked to sit with after midnight, until the waiters started piling chairs on tables, and the taxi drivers left their card games and took their own taxis home.

Serra, as I privately thought of him, was much older than the other men who made up my group of friends. He was in his late sixties, tall for a Spaniard, with facial bones that seemed to carry no flesh but jutted beneath his skin, giving him a slight resemblance to my father, whose bones had also been the most noticeable aspect of his face. But unlike my father, with his almost colorless, sparse hair, Serra had thick, silver hair and skin that was leathery, with deep lines from his nostrils to the corners of his mouth. He smiled a lot, talked little in a group, and was one of the very few men I knew in Figueras who never once betrayed the tiniest hint of flirtation in conversation with me. This was a welcome change from virtually all other male friends and acquaintances who automatically interspersed even serious conversation with sexually suggestive inanities. In Serra, machismo had faded to a low-key chivalry.

From time to time he would give me advice, especially when my romantic dramas reduced me to an exhaustion visible to his perceptive eye. His advice usually involved getting enough sleep and not scandalizing the town any more than I already had by driving home at 4 A.M. with a soldier from the military camp in my passenger seat. Some of this advice, particularly that which related to my nocturnal wanderings, was similar to the advice my father had given a year or two earlier, only when it came from my father it had seemed more like a series of orders. My father had never articulated "consequences" for coming home late, but somehow they had always been there, unnamed in the darkness of the garage when I tried to park the car and close the metal overhead door quietly after midnight—all the while fuming inwardly at being treated like a child.

Serra, however, was a stranger whose advice I could accept with the dignity of an adult since I was free to take it or leave it. Moreover, he was comfortable with me, as if he could see past my Englishness, my blond hair, and the fact that I was as tall as he—all things that caused other Spaniards to regard me as if I were a member of another species. He treated me like a human being with vulnerabilities as well as special qualities, and he was the only one there who did.

Because of this acceptance, I was able to relax with Serra. Everywhere else, I switched personalities from minute to minute, fitting myself in with whatever group or situation I found myself in. At work, for example, I would sometimes have tea in the castle drawing room and then walk back across the road to my office at Las Cavas, effecting a lightning change of personality. From the cautiously sophisticated young woman of the Mateus' drawing room, I transformed myself into a hearty coworker who breezed into the office, slapped Tomás on the back, and cracked a joke about his pile of unfinished paperwork. I had to be good at this because my position in Perclada was quite difficult: although I enjoyed a certain access to the Family (always pronounced by the villagers with a capital letter), clearly I was not one of them. Those men in the office knew, in a way I did not, that everybody ultimately belonged in one camp or the other, and regarded me with suspicion, which spurred on my efforts to fit in.

But though I was comfortable with Serra, there were certain subjects around which I never relaxed, not even with him. One evening, he was sitting at a nearby table while I spent my usual time with the boys at the café. He didn't appear to be listening to our conversation, but I was aware of his presence there when José María and Blanc began discussing the dead soldier who had been found on the road to the military camp. I remember the sudden shift in the tone of their voices, the way they looked furtively right and left, before leaning into the group.

"The body is there on the side of the road," said Alberny,

twisting his hands nervously in a way I had never seen before and didn't understand.

"Aren't they going to bury it?" Blanc asked in horror.

"No, of course not. No one will touch it," snapped Jaime El Rubio.

"But why?" protested Blanc, not getting it. "Why not?"

Eyes shifted uncomfortably. Glances were exchanged. The discomfort was almost audible, a high-pitched discordant whine filling the space around the table and under the sunshade, when finally someone cut through it, muttering: "*¡Era maricón!*" "He was a faggot!" The words seemed to die away with an echo, as two or three other boys concurred under their breaths: "*Maricón—maricón—icón—icón....*"

I felt hot with shame as I sat there not meeting anyone's eyes and resolutely banishing Sophia from my mind. Later, when the boys had left, Serra asked me if everything was all right.

"It seemed as if something unpleasant was said," he ventured.

"Oh no," I replied. "Just boys' stupid jokes," and changed the subject.

Although Serra and I talked often, I really knew very little about him. I never knew, for example, what his work had been before he retired. I discovered that he lived with his mother, who was somewhere between ninety and a hundred, but I never saw her. Ours was a café friendship, at least until it expanded into the teacher/pupil model—but that came later.

Serra would not patronize certain cafés. One such was owned by a stout little man who was reputed to be very wealthy, and who seemed to inspire fear in many of my friends. Once, when I asked about him, José and Isidro looked furtively over their shoulders and muttered something about *la guerra.* A lot of things passed me by, either because of the blithe confidence that makes most of us oblivious of danger at that age, or because I was too ignorant of recent history to pick up on the clues. If I had known more about the war I might even have imagined the disheveled soldiers of the International Brigades walking around my neighborhood as they went through their initial training at Figueras Castle. But back then I knew so little about politics that I barely registered which side the café owner had fought on, even though the *guardias*—Franco's police—often stopped by for a beer and would stand leaning against the whitewashed wall, with their flat-backed shiny hats and polished boots, laughing noisily with their host.

I got to know these same *guardias* rather better when two American boys were involved in a bad car accident on the bypass. Held for hours at the police station, the Americans finally persuaded someone to bring the only person in town who could speak English, and I went to help. The station was dingy and smelly, painted entirely in the dull green of the *guardias'* uniforms and swarming with stray dogs to which the policemen sometimes tossed *patatas fritas* or a well-chewed chop bone. The *guardias* themselves lounged around playing with their guns, twirling them like cowboys or pointing them at each other or at the dogs in mocking gestures reminiscent of small boys. Nobody seemed to do anything much except type with two fingers on an antique typewriter and wait for the call to action. When it came, two or three men would don their hats and sunglasses and emerge, swaggering, into the heat of the day. Swinging their high black boots across their motorcycles, they would roar off in formation.

When I entered the room where the Americans were being

held, three *guardias* were busy taunting the terrified boys, rifling through their personal belongings, threatening physical violence in sign language, and trying to convey the threat that they might hold the boys behind bars indefinitely. I judiciously edited my translation of these remarks and got serious about hiring a lawyer, whereupon the *guardias* lost interest and signed out my grateful new friends upon payment of a stiff, and probably illegal, fine.

Serra was particularly disturbed at this incident, warning me several times to have nothing to do with *guardias*. "They're bad people," he would insist, his brow furrowed with concern, but I didn't understand why I shouldn't interpret for the unfortunate travelers: the police station did not seem so ominous to me, since I knew nothing of the tortures that were part of routine interrogations in the Franco years. Serra could probably have filled me in, but like everyone else who had supported the Republic, he was too nervous to explain anything directly.

One morning, I set off for Perelada a little earlier than usual. The dogs were not yet sprawled in the shade but wandered around with their noses to the ground, stopping now and then to scratch an ear with a back leg. At the first double bend, where the road was rutted from years of cars braking and skidding on the soft tarmac, I noticed a *guardia* standing up on the bank to my left. Keeping my eyes on the bend, which I negotiated with my usual squeal, I thought nothing about the green-clad figure with a gun slung on his back, but simply noted his existence with a displeasure picked up from Serra. In the quarter mile before the next village, I noticed two more, each one lounging against a tree trunk, facing the road. Then, as I roared through the small group of dwellings where people usually waved and shouted at me, there was an odd absence of villagers. There were, however, several more *guardias* on motorcycles, their boots gleaming like the boots of the SS officers in the war movies I had grown up with.

By the time I reached Perelada, it was clear that the whole route was lined with the *Guardia Civil*. Several more stood around the gates into the castle, and I spotted one on top of each of the castle turrets.

"*¿Qué pasa?*" I asked breathlessly at the office.

Tomás looked up from his pile of orders, an enigmatic smile on his face, and said, "It's *El Caudillo*...Franco. He's coming to visit the boss." There was a moment's silence, then Enrique looked up from his ledger and said sarcastically, "Maybe they'll invite you to dinner!"

I knew I was being made fun of but I shrugged it off and spent the rest of the day well away from the castle. That night, when I told Serra about it, he just clicked his teeth, *tsk tsk,* and changed the subject.

AFTER I had known him for a month or two, Serra asked me rather shyly if I would consider teaching him English. He would pay me for the lessons and would find a room where we could meet. Since I liked him and could use the money, I immediately agreed, although I had no textbook and no clear idea of how to plan a course. We started meeting two or three times a week in a small, smoky room at the back of one of the cafés on the *rambla*. Conversation was my main weapon, and I refused to translate my remarks, repeating them until my pupil made a guess and replied hesitantly, using the ten words he had learned at our last meeting. We made slow progress, but Serra seemed satisfied, and as we wandered off for coffee after the lesson, he would relax into confidences about his past.

One night, he told me he had been to England some forty years earlier, in the twenties. "I was a music student," he said. "I studied the cello—such a beautiful instrument. It sings, you know."

He had taken a summer course at Oxford, where he met a young English woman, also a cellist. Obviously something of great significance had happened between them, but he couldn't marry her because he was engaged to a girl back home. The English woman became a friend instead, later visiting him and his wife, who shortly thereafter became mentally ill and was put in a hospital where Serra visited her every Sunday. Had I been the feminist I later became, I probably would have championed the wife in this triangle, but at the time I was a sucker for romance and saw Serra as the victim of a great tragedy. Perhaps he subtly played up this aspect of the story: the young man turning his back on true love to marry his fiancée, who then becomes a burden to him his whole life long. If he did, I didn't notice.

"What was your English friend's name?" I asked him, thoroughly taken with the tale. When he told me, his pronunciation was so bad that I couldn't make it out. It sounded like "Hades," which didn't seem right at all. The third time he said it, he dropped the guttural *jota* and got the G right, at which point I understood her name to be Gladys.

A few weeks later, he invited me to drive with him over the border to Prades, the French Pyrenean village, adopted hometown of Pablo Casals, that hosts an international music festival every summer. Casals, in exile from Spain, had refused to perform in his native country as long as Franco was in power but Prades paid regular tribute to the great cellist and Serra was in the habit of driving up for at least one concert. This year,

Casals, almost ninety, was to play a concerto and Serra had a ticket for me.

In Prades, we pushed our way through a dense crowd of people who would listen to the concert through loudspeakers outside the church. Casals, frail as he was, coaxed his cello into a song that rose, rich and mellow, in the vaults of the church and out into the cobbled streets. After a while, as the hour grew late, the polished pew began to bruise my seat bones, while its stern back relentlessly straightened my sagging spine, but the tones of the cello continued to pour out like a river of oil, soothing, massaging. I shifted my weight on to my left buttock as, suddenly, it occurred to me to write a letter to my mother. There was no one else who would love my description of the music as she would. It was she who had taken me to my first concert—at The Dome in Brighton—when I was five, and to many more in the years that followed. On that first Sunday afternoon, I had seen the great tenor, Peter Pears, and the equally great French horn player, Dennis Brain. My mother had read the program notes with me while the orchestra tuned up, and then withdrawn into wordless contemplation, expecting the same of me.

I jerked out of this reverie with the kind of jolt that wakes you from a dream of falling. My heart was pounding. There would be no letter. I had no mother.

Driving home through the clear night with the top down, the car reflected the moonlight as we climbed steadily toward La Junquera, the air balmy even in the mountains. The melody of *El Cant dels Ocells*—"The Song of the Birds"—still hummed in my ears: that piece Casals played at every concert and referred to as "the theme of the Spanish exiles." The huge night sky shimmered over our heads and we both relaxed into a kind of nostalgia. Presently, I asked Serra if he was still in touch with Gladys.

"Each year at *navidad*, she send letter," he said, in accordance with our agreement to speak English as far as the border. But he couldn't keep it up, and reverted to the Castilian he used with me.

"She has never forgotten me!" he exclaimed with a note of pride in his voice. Then he grew thoughtful and quiet, as we approached the two *guardias* at the frontier post, who might or might not order us out of the car and prod the upholstery with their rifles out of sheer boredom.

IN September that year, I took a week off and met my sister in Barcelona. We drove together to Gibraltar to order a gravestone for our parents—a trip that seemed to occur in a bubble, unconnected to what came before or after. Returning, lonely, from the long drive and Ruth's surprisingly welcome company, I buckled under and worked long hours until the weather broke. As the skies grew heavy with clouds, the tourists flooded into Perelada in one, last, wild orgy of holiday excess, and I started to think about leaving for England. By the second week in October, the grape harvest was safely gathered, the *vendimia* had been celebrated, and I was packing my suitcase to return to England for the winter. I walked out of my hotel after dinner and sat down at a table on the *rambla* to wait for Serra. I had arranged to give him six conversation tapes that I had painstakingly recorded on my little portable tape recorder up in my room during the stifling hours of the siesta.

The nights were still warm, even sultry, but thunder rumbled in the mountains up towards Besalú as storms approached. Soon Serra strolled down the hill with that satisfied look people have at ten or ten-thirty, after a slow dinner with lots of bread and red wine. He sat down carefully and stuck his long legs in their immaculate linen pants out into the street. *"Café solo y un cognac por favor, Jimet,"* he called, and then shifted uncomfortably as if he had something on his mind. I wondered if it had to do with my leaving: perhaps he was about to make one of those Spanish farewell speeches filled with dramatic gestures of sorrow (I'd already received several that day). But he did not. Instead, he reached into his inside pocket and produced a crumpled piece of paper, the kind that comes from spiral bound exercise books in Spain, with little squares instead of lines. On it was written in Serra's spidery script, Gladys Welford's London address.

"I thought perhaps you might go and visit her," he explained, "that is, if you have time."

He hesitated, sensing I would require some reason for such a visit, and went on: "I would very much like you to meet her and convey my best wishes. I do not suppose we will ever meet again, she and I."

I knew it had already been thirty years or so since Gladys had last visited Serra and his wife, who, at that time, had been well enough to be living temporarily at home. And Serra had never returned to England after that one Oxford summer. It did, indeed, seem unlikely that these star-crossed lovers, if that's what they were, would ever set eyes on each other again.

I took the paper and said I would look her up, and Serra seemed glad to change the subject. He referred to it just once more when he said much later, as we were leaving the square: "You will write to me if you see Gladys." It was a statement, not a question, and I just nodded.

Which is why, one Sunday afternoon in late October, I found

myself walking through a quiet part of Chelsea north of the King's Road, a crumpled piece of paper and an *A to Z* street guide in my hand. I had tried to find a phone number for Gladys Welford, but none had been listed, so I was hoping I would find her at home and receptive to my visit. Judging from the neighborhood, Gladys had done well for herself. Had she married someone wealthy? Had she become a famous cellist? How had she come to belong in these tree-lined streets of Georgian houses with gardens that were lovely even now with the fallen leaves adding an exuberant disarray to the flower beds.

In those days I looked at my life as if it were a novel or a movie, in which I was the star. Perhaps I was trying to comfort myself, or maybe just distract myself, by making up a version of events that was by turns intriguing, glamorous, or dramatic. I wove imaginative tales around the people of Figueras, the villagers at Perelada, the tourists at the beach, and, now—trudging through those Chelsea streets—around Sr. Serra's long-ago romance with Gladys Welford. These stories kept me living in a present I could make up as I went along; there was no room in them for the past. It was like a story narrated in the present tense: impossible to shape in all its fullness because of the difficulty of moving back and forth in time. The language itself, like heavy mud, sucks at your feet and weighs your story down.

As I walked, I worked on the myth: Gladys must be about the same age as Serra, I reasoned, since they were on the same course at Oxford. Perhaps she was in some kind of retirement home. Or perhaps one of these elegant pillared houses was a genteel nursing home where she could be in any stage of ill-health. What if she didn't even remember Serra?

The street, when I found it, was very narrow with a high

brick wall running the entire length of the block on the north side. Ivy, beginning to turn red, clung to the crumbling mortar, and halfway along the wall was an archway with a heavy wooden door bearing the number on my piece of paper. I could barely see the large building behind the wall as I pulled the iron handle and heard a bell jangle inside. After a few minutes the door opened, revealing a shady garden, and a very correct, starched nun fixed me with a gaze. "Yes?" she said. I was still thinking nursing home, as I explained that I would like to visit Gladys Welford, and that if this was not a good time I could return another day.

"Follow me," said the nun curtly, turning up the gravel path, between heavily laden apple trees, to the front door of the square building, also ivy-covered. Somewhere to my right, I heard water trickling, as if there were a small fountain. The Kings Road, the shouts from the pubs, and the traffic of Chelsea already seemed so far away, I doubted they would still be there if I turned and went out again through the wooden door.

In the tiled entrance hall, a crucifix hung in an alcove below the staircase. I sat on a wooden bench, noticing how polished everything was—wood, brass, tile, even the leading around the stained glass window halfway up the stairs. It all smelled of lemon and warm oil. Presently another nun, friendlier and plumper that the first, came and stood in front of me. "Sister Mary Margaret will be able to meet with you in about fifteen minutes if you don't mind waiting," she smiled.

"Sister Mary Margaret?" I repeated, wondering if this was someone whose job it was to break the news of Gladys's dire condition to me.

"You were asking for her, I believe," the nun said gently,

waiting for me to make the connection. Gladys Welford was not a patient in a nursing home; she was Sister Mary Margaret.

I waited, my mind racing. Had Serra known that Gladys was a nun? If so, why hadn't he told me? Surely she couldn't have written to him each year at Christmas without letting slip this rather important fact about herself. Was he embarrassed? Did he take it to mean that he had broken her heart, and was my visit a small penance on his part? Or had she hidden the convent from him to protect him from such thoughts?

Gladys—or Sister Mary Margaret—and I chatted in a small reception room for about forty-five minutes. Someone brought a tray of tea and four pieces of shortbread, and Gladys handled the teapot as if she received visitors all the time. She was serene and rather formal, sitting upright with her hands folded, except when one slid smoothly out to hold her shortbread and lift it to her lips for a small bite, carefully replacing the remainder on its willow-pattern plate, and returning the hand to its mate among the black folds of her lap. But, in spite of this formality, there was a twinkle in her expression that matched the laugh lines around her faded blue eyes. When I told her I knew Señor Serra, she inclined her head gravely but said nothing. When I conveyed his best wishes, she smiled a little and asked if he was well. "Oh yes," I exclaimed. "He's wonderful for his age: very upright, very well-dressed. He has a great zest for life."

Then I told her about our lessons and his enthusiasm for learning, and she asked precisely how I had gone about teaching him English. We might have been discussing a distant acquaintance of hers for all the emotion she betrayed—or did her voice shake just a little when, finally, she looked up quickly and asked, "And his wife? Is she still so ill?"

I nodded. "I've never met her, I'm afraid, but I believe she has no hope of recovery." I sounded to myself as if I were acting in a film from the forties. I glanced at Gladys, who was putting the tea things back on the tray. The cups were both rattling on their saucers and her hands were shaking. She placed the blue cups carefully next to the shortbread plate, sat up very straight, and looked at me with her mouth set in a firm line. There was a pause and then her voice burst through those tight lips, bitter and wild, as if it had unwittingly escaped the confines of her carefully composed face, her taut, white wimple, and the ivy-covered walls that surrounded her life. "And I suppose you think he's been a saint, like all the rest of them!"

She gave me no time to reply, which was fortunate as I was profoundly silenced. Instead, she put her face back together and politely indicated that our discussion was over. The sense of being in a movie grew stronger. Now was the time for the background music to fade in as she walked me slowly to the front door: tasteful music, perhaps a Beethoven quartet, as we crossed the garden, she in front in her black and white habit, me behind in my good camel coat. Then the camera would pull back and back, zooming high up into the air until we were just two distant figures walking among a profusion of autumn fruits and burnished leaves, in a patchwork of streets intersected by the river.

Gladys swung the wooden door open and the noise of the city burst in. I stumbled out of the film and over the step. The gate closed behind me, and, as the latch clicked into place, I turned, wanting to call her back. "What did you mean?" I would demand. "Of course he's a good man." But I was left standing outside that solid stone wall with only the memory of Gladys Welford's brittle cry and the disturbing sensation that Sr. Serra might belong in an entirely different story from the one I had made up for him.

In the dim, leathery pub on King's Road, I tried to put Gladys's wild anger out of my mind, but I couldn't forget her shaking hands. Drumming my foot against the front of the bar, I moved my thoughts firmly into the present, ordered another beer, and addressed my postcard to Serra. *I've seen Gladys,* I wrote. *She remembers you very well.*

Exhalations

IN MAY 1965, I RETURNED TO Perelada after my first winter break in England. Sometimes it still seemed as if I hadn't been able to breathe since that Christmas, a year and a half earlier, when I had held my breath for so long, waiting for news of my parents. Driving to work, I would feel the hot air rush past my nose and mouth, but it never reached deep into my lungs and belly. I was holding on too tight for that.

It was particularly noticeable when I got sick. In July, lying in bed with an escalating temperature, I could hear the shallow breaths rasping, as if they were running across the teeth of a comb lodged in my throat. The fever went on day after day, and I lay in my cell-like room in the Hotel Paris, the starched white sheets growing limp and grey, the ruckus from the street three floors down invading my room through the shutters. On market day it was awful. Everyone screamed and bellowed: little kids playing, grown men arguing, women going about their business—raucous ¡hola!s and ¿qué tal?s followed by streams of high-pitched Catalan as they swapped the latest news or bargained for a kilo of snails. I glared at the ceiling and mapped the cracks in the plaster.

Maybe Señor Fernando carried a bowl of vermicelli broth up to my room. Probably he sent a maid. Or maybe I just didn't eat. I didn't want to read. I had no music. And I'm sure I didn't think too much. I might have written a line or two of a feverish letter to Sophia. Probably I thought about calling her on the telephone, but that would never have worked. International calls happened at the *teléfonos* building and you had to wait hours for your call to be placed. I couldn't do that lying in bed with a fever. Throwing the damp sheet aside, I remembered my mother's claim that Franco had improved the telephone service. What could she have been thinking? Everyone in Figueras knew it was quicker to drive the five hundred miles to Madrid than to wait for a phone connection.

Mostly what I remember are the clocks. Church clocks. Four of them. Naturally they were not synchronized. So the first one, just the other side of the market square, started off bonking the hour and then the second one joined in while the first was still going. The third one, which had a sweet tone like a carillon, only overlapped the first two if it was an hour with a lot of chimes like eleven or twelve. Otherwise it struck alone, melodious and blessedly distant, while the reverberations of the first two were still vibrating in my iron bedstead. The fourth was a straggler, limping in like the horse that finished twenty lengths behind. Nevertheless I waited for it, hating myself for my crazy need to anticipate its first tinny note.

The fever was burning me up, people were crashing in and out of my dreams, only I wasn't asleep, and the clocks never stopped. Soon the first clock was starting to chime hard on the heels of the fourth clock. The quarter started while the hour itself was just fading. Half past and quarter till merged together until every hour was filled with bells. First it was the old St. Mary's Hall school bell with the bronze clapper that summoned us in from breaktime all through the fifties. No matter which beautiful senior was on duty at the time, standing up on the top terrace in her snowy white blouse, lifting the bell in the air, and sweeping it back and forth, we gazed up at her from the lawns as if at a goddess. Then came the St. Mark's Church bell, next door to the school, intersecting the day with dreadful regularity. But worst of all was the sober bell of All Saints', Patcham, ringing from its square Norman tower. All Saints' was the one that reproached my mother when she forgot to change the clocks at the end of daylight savings time and walked up the path to the church door an hour late. It was also the one that summoned me to my wedding as I rode in the back of the black Rolls Royce in my white dress up the hill under those ominous oak trees—but no, that hadn't happened yet! That was still four years in the future, though maybe in my fever I foresaw it—who knows? I was in Figueras with a temperature of 104 degrees, not married yet, but somehow I knew those bells would ring for me one day soon. They would let out thunderous peals of celebration as I emerged from the church and posed as a wife in front of the cameras. Bells for the marriage that wouldn't last a year. But now they were tolling for all those Sundays my parents, my brother and sister, and I didn't show up, and for the Christmas mornings we did. They were tolling because I loved to hear church bells, especially across green meadows through clear, cool air—not this feverish air, dense with oaths and eau de cologne. I liked to watch a small crowd of the faithful wending its way towards the sound of the bells, like children following the Pied Piper, while I stayed out there in the lush meadows, immune to the spell.

The air in my room was hot and thick and that bell wouldn't stop. Now it was the All Saints' of eighteen months ago: January 2nd, 1964. It was 2:30 and Ruth and John and I were in the front pew. The Reverend Garston-Smith was talking about my parents. Then we were singing *oh hear us when we cry to thee for those in peril on the sea* and the bell was ringing one note, bong bong bong. The one-note dirge, like the single bell that tolls on Sunday mornings after the great, repeating, downward cascade of peals has died away: the dirge of the one repeated note that means you are late. It was tolling now through my Figueras window and I suspected I was late. Late to church, late to the wedding, late to the tears.

I GOT sick a lot when I lived in Figueras. It didn't usually last as long as that fever, nor did I usually consider it legitimate enough to stay in bed. In fact, I didn't pay much attention to it back then, but it's all recorded in those little diaries I kept at the time: tiny datebooks that were meant for two appointments a day, but which I used instead to record all the day's events. No feelings. Just facts. The writing is so small, I have to wear reading glasses to decipher it, and even with glasses sometimes I can't make it out. Mostly it's just things like *Work was boring. Big group of Germans visited. Drinks with Alberny and the gang after dinner. Granny's with Jaime. Back late.* Not much more than that would fit, even when I wrote so small it looked as if the words couldn't possibly be made up of individual letters.

There were codes too. Secret things having to do with Sophia. Sometimes I wrote *Got a letter* and didn't have to say from whom. Then there was that crazy time, halfway through the summer, when I drove back to England for the weekend. I thought I would die if I didn't go back and see her, although I was supposed to be working in Perelada at a job where people expected me to show up Monday through Friday and sometimes Saturday. But I behaved then like I behave now if I've got to do something that other people won't understand. Or if I don't understand it myself. I simply acted as if I didn't have to explain. It was like that a few years later, when I left Colin ten months after marrying him. I couldn't explain that to anyone—not myself, not my family, not him, though I tried. "He hit me," I said, but I knew that was only a small and fairly irrelevant part of the story. I just didn't know the rest yet. So when I rushed off to England from Perelada that summer, I simply said, "Something came up. Be back on Tuesday." And I took off.

The diary doesn't say much about that trip: *July 21: Up 4 am. Drove and drove! Breakfast in Cahors. Slept in a wood. Arrived Dieppe 10.05 pm. Rang S. Left car in garage. July 22: Got ferry 1.15 am. Sea rough. Arrived Newhaven 5 am. S picked me up. Went to bed. Then out in country. Leaves falling.*

Driving back south to Figueras after that long weekend was not as easy as the impulsive journey north had been. I was tired and lonely. I sighed a lot, as if something was trying to get out of my body on the back of the exhaled breath. It might have been those images from the Christmas of my parents' death—

the leering, red face of the pantomime villain and a theatre-full of children hissing every time he came on stage; the audience panic as our hero (was it Peter Pan?) failed to notice the danger and the smallest toddlers yelled out, beside themselves with delicious fear, "Watch out—he's right behind you!" Or it might have been the telephoning every hour in the little closet under the stairs with the vacuum cleaner and hundreds of clothespins and the recorded list of names playing over and over. Entering that closet, we all held our breath. Who knew if the others had started to breathe again? I hadn't.

But the diary says nothing of all that. It simply records my times of arrival at key points in the journey—something I recently realized was not unlike my father's compulsive trip planning. The day I got back, having driven all day and all night, I slotted right back in as if nothing had happened. *July 27: Arrived Figueras 11.00 am. Unpacked. Sent telegram. 1 hr. siesta. To work. Drank champagne. Bed 1.*

The diary never explains about getting sick. There are just days that say: *Felt dreadful. Stayed in bed.* And when I look at more of those little books, I find the same thing in the years that followed: 1968; 1969; 1971: years when I was working in offices in London; years when I was living in a women's collective: *Felt dreadful. Stayed in bed.* Some of the entries refer to migraines. A lot, especially in Figueras, were hangovers. From champagne, brandy, wine, cigarettes, and from going on and on and never sleeping.

I don't use those tiny datebooks anymore—don't record a whole day in a half inch of white space that guarantees I won't say anything I shouldn't. Now I have a loose-leaf journal. No days marked on it, just lined sheets of paper so a day can take thirty pages if it wants. But I still have those *felt dreadful, stayed in bed* days. Sometimes they're migraines. But never hangovers. At least not from alcohol. Maybe from work. What I really think is that they're hangovers of sadness or anger and that they probably always have been. There's a pain in the head like an auger drilling behind one eye and sometimes a bit of throwing up too.

Most people don't have safe opportunities to feel. I certainly didn't—not there in Figueras, and not back in England either, where it had seemed to me that no one wanted me to feel bad around them. My family and friends had seemed as embarrassed as I was about being connected to such a dramatic, public spectacle. If you store it up every time something horrible happens to you, or every time you see someone starving or beating a child or going berserk in the way people do, what with wars and families and loneliness and all the rest, it stands to reason it's going to do something to your body sooner or later.

Sometimes the Figueras diary says *felt dreadful* but does not say *stayed in bed*. This was because I was afraid I was a hypochondriac and needed to pretend I was all right. On days like that, I avoided coffee because it smelled like poison. I took a bottle of mineral water along with me and drove the winding road to work carefully, making sure my stomach kept up with the car as I negotiated the bends and tilted over the humpbacked bridges with unusual caution. But people would notice my pasty face.

"¡Ay, Judith!" said Tomás in the office. "Too much cognac!"

"¡Ay, Judith!" said Rosé at the bar. "So many boys! You have to sleep!"

"¡Ay, Judith!" said Carmen in the castle drawing room, "¡No es fácil la vida! Life's not easy!"

This last analysis seemed to come closest but lacked specificity. I had no idea what I needed, but in retrospect I wish I had met just one person who wanted to know about my parents. Not about their tragic death—I had plenty of people throwing their hands in the air at the horror of that—but about who they had been when they were alive. Surely it was by remembering them alive that I would open the stubborn door to sadness. Neither my brother nor my sister seemed able to talk about them, and people like my mother's best friend, Germaine, thought they could protect me by pretending, when I was around, that my parents had never existed.

One way of dealing with feeling dreadful was to show up for work, just to keep things looking right, but to make up fictitious appointments. "Some friends of our London importer have arrived in San Feliú," I would say casually, leafing through a pile of letters in the office, as if one of them had given me this piece of information. "I'd better go down there and introduce myself. They'll be wanting to come up here sometime soon."

And with that I would get into my car and be gone. Sometimes I went down to the beach, if my headache allowed me to be in the sun. There I lay like a stranded jellyfish, sprawled on the sand, face down. The sun enveloped me in a protective cocoon, while the screams of tourists and the regular crash of small waves sounded distant, as if behind a screen of thick glass. Somewhere up the hill, the inevitable church bell would strike the quarters as I buried my face in a beach towel and felt waves of what I thought was nausea, but which was probably just plain misery, wash over and through me.

At other times I couldn't stand the rawness of the beach, choosing instead to stop somewhere along the road and lie down in the shade of the pine trees. Mediterranean pines always smelled good—almost medicinal—in their aromatic intensity. To lie under those scrubby trees, looking straight up through their emerald, long-needled branches at the expanse of blue was soothing. The domed sky was a cradle. There was enough vast space up there to dissipate whatever poison I was carrying in my insignificant body. I was only an ant. A speck. My breathing in and out was simply a part of the whole, great mechanism, as was each pine needle that collected dew to nourish a wind-battered tree, which, in turn exhaled into the great blue atmosphere as I did.

My heartbeat quieted after a while. Then I would roll over and bury my face in the bed of needles, wondering if the trees, too, had days like this, days when their exhalations were full of miseries—all the miseries the winds picked up and blew relentlessly across the wide Ampurdán plain.

Dream Time

AT THREE OR FOUR IN THE afternoon, you open your eyes from a heavy, dreamless sleep, aware of your lunch still lying in your stomach. Your skin is slightly damp from the sweat of sleep. The sheets are limp. Your room is dark, its dim space giving an illusion of coolness that doesn't hold up to scrutiny, especially when you turn toward the shutters, which do not quite meet in the middle of the window. There, through the crack, a narrow band of sun, so bright as to be pure, colorless light, enters the room at an angle and crosses to the far wall, slicing the bottom of your bed on its way. If you throw aside the sheet and put your foot there, where the sunbeam touches the bed, you can feel the intense heat on your ankle bone and the tender skin above your toes.

Waking from a siesta, your mouth feels dry, your brain

sodden, as if you'll never make a witty remark again. Some-times, as you surface from an unconsciousness that is sticky and thick like molasses, you have no idea where you are or what day it is—perhaps even your own name is gone. When that happens, your stomach lurches and you feel unbalanced, as if you are falling. You reach out a hand and grasp the marble top of the bedside table, holding on as if it had the power to restore all the lost equilibrium of the world. Everything shifts sideways; your name slips into its slot; it's Wednesday after-noon and you'd better get back to work.

In Figueras, I would wake from siesta and wander out into the *rambla* for a cup of coffee, before driving back down the road to Perelada. As I stepped out of the hotel, I felt the after-noon warmth wrap me in its embrace. Unlike the morning sun, with its stunning blow of greeting, the afternoon heat was mis-leading in its softness, its ability to seep into your bones with-out scorching your surfaces. I would sit under an umbrella, waiting for my coffee, still three-quarters asleep, and breathe the essence of this time of day into my lungs.

Sometimes, when I decided to skip siesta, I would linger in Perelada as the village drifted into the stillness of the lunch hour. Trucks would wait at the loading docks as the heat gradually built towards afternoon. Excited voices from the office and chatter from the bar faded away. A fly zoomed past my ear as I leaned back against the crumbling wall to make way for a cart pulled by two oxen piled high with grapes in wooden vats. Perelada didn't look very different than I imag-ine it looked in the sixteenth century. Back then most of the houses would have been the same ones I saw now, and the Carmelite convent, whose roof I glimpsed over the castle wall, would already have been more than two centuries old. True, in the sixteenth century there was no modern wine factory, none of the wires draped from flat roof to flat roof, and no television aerials scrawling their angular graffiti against the sky. But still, the cart that rumbled past me might have been on that road for five hundred years or more.

As drivers and loaders left for their lunch, I wandered through the little garden catching a glimpse of Martín, one of the seventy-year-old brothers who worked in the castle, Martín as librarian and Pedro as major-domo. Neither of them ever went to Barcelona. In fact, they rarely left the castle grounds, finding no reason to visit Figueras, five miles to the southwest, much less the coast, fifteen miles to the east. The very idea of Pedro and Martín, in their shabby black suits, rubbing shoulders with the tourists in Cadaqués was preposterous.

When the streets were empty, I would set off to the beach by the winding back road, passing through Garriguella just as the one little store was closing its shutters for a nap. At Rosas, I would run across the burning sand in front of the Hotel Marian and dive into the water, which would close over my head and welcome me into its green belly. The ocean was so clear, I could see every rock, every stray little fish, every strand of weed waving as I floated by. The touch of that cool, soft water was not unlike the touch of the sun. It loosened all my muscles; soothed everything into place.

If I didn't bump into any friends—a circumstance that became rarer and rarer I would emerge from the water and throw myself down onto a beach towel, burying my head in my arms, lulled by the breaking waves and the shouts of holidaymakers playing ball. The heat was fierce, but I knew how to give in to it, deflecting its bite so it washed over my limp body with a suffused warmth in the midst of which I grew sleepy. Then I would smile secretly into the dark space created by the circle of my arms.

Sometimes, although not quite asleep, I dreamed as one does at siesta time. Often, I found myself in England in my mother's garden, while she pottered around with her trug over her arm, and chalky earth on her hands. I saw her stooping from her great height to pull a weed or pinch back a lettuce. I saw her sunburnt, nut-brown arms, and the white lines around her eyes where she had screwed them up against the sun. Then the dream would switch to flying. I would be in a plane, skimming very low over the ocean, rising and falling with the contours of the great swells.

I would stand up too quickly, my head spinning, and drag my towel towards me, fine sand powdering my feet as they groped their way into sandals. At the outdoor bar of the Hotel Marian, I sat on my usual bar stool, drinking a coke—the only thing I was willing to pay for on these excursions. The rest of my lunch consisted of crispy bread rolls from the basket on the bar, which were supposed to accompany one of the lunches: chicken from the spit, *calamares* deep fried in light batter, or a tough piece of steak with french fries. I only ever ate the *calamares,* which were so delicious they seemed somehow to transcend mere food, and only then when someone treated me. My employers picked up the tab for my hotel in Figueras, no matter how extravagant my meals, but anything I ate elsewhere was my problem. And I was getting virtually no salary.

It was over these slow, carbohydrate lunches that I met Pepe, a waiter at the Hotel Marian. In retrospect, my relationship with him seems entirely reflective of the time of day that we met. It was a sleepy relationship. My dreams were more present than the bar and the ferns and the persistent murmur of German and French conversations in the background.

Pepe was long-legged and a bit ungainly like a colt, but very appealing to look at with his wide mouth and brown, floppy hair that overlapped his white waiter's collar by an inch at the back. He was not Catalan but had come north from his home somewhere near Granada to make some fast money over the summer. He bustled about behind the bar, twitching the caps off coke bottles, shaking up cocktails, and bringing out lunches six at a time on a tray he held high as he wound his way between tables and large potted plants. Once in a while, when the manager was gone, he would slip me a plate of *calamares*, but when I realized he was risking his job, I went back to the bread. It was Pepe who suggested that ketchup and mustard would liven up the bread rolls, as he scooted the condiments down the bar towards me. After that, I always spread one half of each roll with thick red and smeared the other with yellow— and he was right: it was much more lively.

When he wasn't busy, Pepe would stand in front of my half-asleep, bikini-clad body, salt-encrusted and glowing from the sun, and talk at me. Most of his conversation washed over me as the green sea and the sun had a few minutes earlier. Words, few of which I grasped, swam past at a great distance, though I managed to nod and grunt as if I were a participant. This is probably why things moved much faster than they would have if I had been paying proper attention, so that one afternoon I found myself listening to Pepe unravel his plan for our evening date. I couldn't recall any discussion about the date, but I supposed I must have assented to it by grunting at the wrong moment, since the plan was already well developed. I was to meet him when he finished work at eleven that night and he would take me out dancing.

The siesta mentality, passive, even lethargic as it was, was actually only an exaggerated version of my general attitude: I took the line of least resistance, without really considering my options. That's how I ended up at a great many nightclubs with a variety of men I didn't choose.

Pepe, it turned out, had an agenda, as I found out that night about midnight after we had danced up a sweat at Granny's and retreated to the beach. We sat on an upturned boat under the stars, whose shimmering seemed exactly to match the trilling of the cicadas. I reminded myself that the stars, as far as I knew, were silent, and that the chorus of rasping song was coming from the grass behind the beach and not from the pinpoints of light above. I wondered when Pepe was going to make his move.

But Pepe had more in mind than a quick grope behind a boat. Before I knew it, he was down on one knee asking me to marry him. He wanted to go to England with me, he said. First he would take me to meet his family. He would get a better job in England. And, he added as romantically as he could, he loved me.

I was speechless. My first response was to pretend it hadn't happened and to pull him up off the sand and try to seduce him. Maybe he just felt he had to prove he was serious before he started to remove any clothing. But he wouldn't go along with it. He didn't mind a bit of kissing, but he wasn't going any further. So I said no. I was perfectly clear: I wasn't going to marry him. Not now. Not ever.

This happened at the end of September. I tried to avoid Pepe until early November, when I returned to England for the winter, my second season at Perelada completed. The day after I crossed the Channel from Dieppe, I was walking down

Eastern Road in Brighton when I turned and bumped right into Pepe. He had followed me by train to London, then gone all the way to Bristol before finding his way to Brighton because he had mispronounced the word when buying his ticket. I was furious with him. In fact I lost my temper right there in the street.

"What do you think you're doing?" I yelled. "I said no, didn't I? What do you want from me?"

But I knew what he wanted. He had that hangdog look men get when they are smitten. Reluctantly, I took him to my apartment and put him up there for a couple of nights, giving him frequent lectures about leaving. Perhaps because of the constant rain, there was nothing that remotely resembled siesta-time, and I quickly became unrecognizable to Pepe. There were no long, lazy discussions during which I grunted and he waved his hands; no brushing of bare arm against bare arm, the skin receptive and sensitized by its exposure to water and air. And—what seemed to frighten him the most—I was one hundred percent wide awake the whole time.

Pepe left on a train very soon afterwards. I waved him off, seeing the disappointment in his face as he leaned out of the window, his arm lifted in a slightly ironic salute. Of course I felt guilty at my lack of vigilance. It was my drowsiness back there at the bar of the Hotel Marian that had allowed Pepe to fall in love with a zombie who was not me—or at least was only me from two to three in the afternoon in a hot climate. But, once his train pulled away out of sight, it all faded very quickly until, a few weeks later, it might have been a dream. A siesta dream, heavy and deep. A dream you wake from, tired and slightly grouchy, with no recollection of where you have been. And no idea at all why you went there.

Sleeping Around

IN FIGUERAS I SLEPT WITH A lot of men. Or, to be more accurate, I was sexual with a lot of men: I never actually spent a night with one. I was terrified of getting pregnant, which I dealt with by insisting that the sex be more or less anything but straightforward penetration. There was a lot of groping and rolling around on my bed, or someone else's, with a messy, always furtive, moment of ecstasy on the part of Fernando or Francisco or Federico, that spilled sometimes on to my bare, tanned stomach and sometimes on to the starched, linen bedspread or the orange and blue beach towel. One might expect men to find this annoying, but I always got my way.

Take, for example, the Italians—three of them—I met one night in Puerto de la Selva. A lot of brandy blurred the events at the time as well as in my memory now, but looking back on it I am more than a little surprised that I didn't get raped when I ended up in the back seat of a very small Fiat with one of them, while the other two jerked off in the front seats.

Then there was the policeman—not a *guardia* but one of the numerous other kinds of police—I met in the small village of Garriguella at the Molí de Ven, the old windmill that an enterprising young couple, Ramón and María, had converted into a very popular disco. The latest hits pounded their beat through the musty alcoves, with rickety wooden tables and candles dripping down the sides of Mateus Rose bottles, and out into the vast night, throbbing with cicadas. I drove to the Molí around precipitous, hairpin bends, as Dusty's voice rolled out in wave after wave across sagebrush and rock, "I Only Want to Be with You" scattering the lizards into dried-up gullies.

Once again, too much brandy accompanied my dancing with the policeman—or to be more accurate, standing up with him and having foreplay to the music. When he took me outside and leaned me up against a Mediterranean pine, I was, as usual, compliant up to a point. When his hand went inside my underwear I didn't object; but when he tried to replace it with his penis, I strenuously wiggled away. Spanish men, it seems, were used to this foreign standard. Without comment, he made do with my thighs and it was all over in about three minutes.

It is rather shocking to me now, looking back on all that groping, that I had no sense of my own pleasure. I was not doing it for sexual gratification—indeed, I was abysmally ignorant in that area, and had only recently uttered the word orgasm for the first time with Sophia, the lover I had left behind in Wales. My need to witness each man's desire might have marked me for a whore—or, since I wasn't paid, at least a very loose woman—had it not been for an odd kind of prudishness, which kept me from acknowledging what was really going on, even while it was going on. I didn't flirt or seduce—or if I did, I didn't do it intentionally; I merely let the sex happen and tried to keep my dignity in the process.

I was in a world where neither grief, nor sadness, nor any real sense of loss could touch me, intoxicated by the power of my blond hair and long legs over all these men, distracted by the romantic notion of living alone in a small Spanish town, and anesthetized by the alcohol I used to fuel a fantasy life—the only life I could afford to live. I was aware of only one sadness: the absence of the woman who had seduced me a couple of months earlier. That pain was as intense as the Catalan midday sun. Had I been able to speak of it, I would have said that I doubted I could survive without her.

I had created not one but two distractions from grief: an intense affair with a woman, doomed to secrecy and disaster, and a series of meaningless sexual encounters with men. My heart remained besieged by the first, while my body was assaulted by the second. They both worked, as narcotics work, for a while. Still, my need for distraction was a daily, hourly thing. I drank, worked, danced, drove my sports car, and picked up men at every turn as if it were the only possible way of life.

I met Andrés at a café where I knew most of the regulars, and where he came occasionally for a cognac and coffee after dinner. I knew virtually nothing about him except that he was a jeweller and that he wanted to take me around and be seen in my company. He was more than old enough to be my father, unattractive, uninteresting, not particularly nice to me, and impotent. His impotence was about the most sexually interesting thing I encountered that whole summer. His inability to perform made me feel extremely safe, as well as more sexual than I felt with other men, and I took guilty pleasure in displaying my body on his bed in the small, back-street *pensión* where he lived.

It was Andrés who introduced me to Figueras's only cinema, which reeked of garlic and showed mostly cowboy movies dubbed into Spanish, seen through a thick cloud of pungent cigarette smoke. When some traveling variety show passed through town, he took me to the theater. As the nearly naked chorus girls danced across the stage, he seized my hand and pressed it to his swelling erection which, as usual, failed to materialize later in his room. My friends from the café, who warned me against Andrés, were worried more about my reputation than my safety. I gathered he was a bit of a rake, that he frequented the town's many brothels, and that he was considered slightly unsavory—not because of the brothels, which many of the boys and men I knew patronized, but because he displayed his sexual obsessions in public in a way that was unacceptable for a man close to sixty.

For a few weeks I ignored the advice and wandered regularly over to his *pensión* as if in a trance. He probably thought I would employ some practiced sex tricks to turn him on, but such a thing never occurred to me, and if it had, I wouldn't have known how. I merely admired my own young body and enjoyed feeling sinful, while he stormed around in a fury that I did not understand. When he presented me with a ring and a gold watch, I accepted the gifts, feeling elated at behaving like a kept woman.

The effect of my sleazy behavior was to obliterate everything but the present moment: it blotted out my longing for Sophia's arms, her voice murmuring into my receptive ear, her hands roaming my utterly responsive skin. Beyond that, it blotted out the great and awful fact of being alone in the world before I had even realized that such a thing could happen.

THE only men I didn't have sex with were the men who didn't try. As I think back on it, they divide up fairly evenly into those who chose to be friends of some sort, and those with whom I had an affair. The group of boys I hung out with at the café were all in the first category, even José María, who had only briefly flirted with the idea of joining the second. Arturo Suqué, my handsome employer, also maintained a careful distance, though I often expected and sometimes hoped for him to cross the line.

In truth, most of the flirting I did was with women—something that seemed quite acceptable there, where young girls wandered arm in arm or held hands before dinner in the *rambla*. I thrilled to the intense interest, flattery, and sensuous caresses of my hairdresser, Rosa, and the less obvious, but nevertheless intense, attraction between me and Arturo Suqué's wife, Carmen.

Carmen Mateu de Suqué, the pampered daughter of one of Spain's richest families, was unlike any of the women I had met in Figueras. She was some eight years older than I and beautiful in a fragile way. Sometimes she lived in the castle with her three young children and a large staff of servants, who deprived her of any tasks other than embroidery or letter writing; sometimes she migrated down to the villa on the headland at Garbet, or to the mansion in Barcelona. No matter where she was, she was lonely and bored to the point of developing imaginary symptoms for which she was sent to a Swiss heart specialist several times.

The first time she invited me over to the castle for tea, I crossed the road and pulled the secret knob to open the little door set into the studded entrance gates. The gatekeeper summoned a servant, who led me into the courtyard and then down a series of hallways to the drawing room. Carmen, whom I'd met out in the garden a couple of times, leaped out of a red velvet chair and shook my hand, turning to introduce me to her mother, a woman I would come to think of as "the old lady."

Almost a caricature of the aristocrat, Señora Mateu stared haughtily at me down her hooked nose and extended a bony hand; right away she scared me to death. Another servant brought in a trolley with *merienda*—bread with tomato and an assortment of cakes accompanied by some kind of flowery tea. Balancing my fine china plate on my knee and trying to cut tomato-soaked bread with a gold knife inlaid with the Perelada coat-of-arms, I weighed up the relative merits of speaking with my mouth full or requiring the old lady to wait for an answer as she questioned me closely about my job. Only later would I realize the extent of her disapproval, particularly when I started bringing tourists around the castle grounds. Time and again she would send Pedro, the major-domo, to tell me that it was "not a convenient time" and in the end I gave in and held off from taking the big groups inside the castle walls until the family was away. I had to learn to coexist with this autocratic matriarch, whose presence in the castle cast a pall over the entire village.

After that first time, Carmen and I would meet alone in one of the smaller rooms and exchange tentative stories about our families, but even when it was just the two of us it seemed as if the portraits on the walls were assessing our conversation. I remember her telling me about her wedding, on the occasion of which her father had had a hole knocked through the north wall of the dining hall—six feet thick and solid stone—and the long oak dining table extended into a marquee to accommodate a couple of hundred extra guests. Arturo, she said, had laid down a special batch of Perelada's best red wine with a commemorative label dedicated to Queen Fabiola of Belgium, who had been the guest of honor. This kind of talk, particularly when it took place in the castle, was out of my league.

One day I got a call from her when she was down at the Garbet villa. It came through to the Perelada office, where I took it self-consciously in front of Enrique and Tomás, whose communist politics led them to express grave disapproval whenever I hobnobbed with "the family." Would I like to come down tomorrow for the day? she asked. There was nobody there except her and the children, a nanny and some servants. She was going crazy, she said.

It was never really clear who was my immediate boss at the winery. Officially, I reported to Señor Dominguez, whose office was at the shop in Figueras, so I rarely saw him, except to pick up some money now and then. But out at Perelada, I operated independently, which disturbed just about everyone. Carmen's mother, for example, thought I should arrange everything having to do with tours of the castle grounds with her, or with someone connected to her household, but not with Arturo, whose ridiculous idea it had been in the first place to hire me. The manager of the wine business, Señor Ríos, felt the same way about the visitors who trudged through the cellars; he expected me to ask him before I ushered them down the staircase into the dimly lit catacombs with their bins of dusty green bottles and huge oak vats. But I never asked permission for anything, choosing, rather, to wait until someone complained. I had been told to create my own job, and I was doing just that. So when Carmen invited me down to the coast for the day, I assumed her status as a member of the family warranted my immediate acceptance.

I arrived about eleven in the morning, after an exhilarating drive over the mountains and along the winding coast road. As I skidded around each hairpin bend, a new vista opened out, with what looked like a bottomless, dark green bay, almost a lagoon, enclosed within the embrace of two rocky arms, on my right. To the left, the hills rose abruptly, sprouting cacti and small flowers and an occasional olive grove. For the last few miles, I could see the Mateu villa, perched on a headland, the hillside below carefully tiered and cultivated with vines. As I approached, swinging round bends, sometimes doubling back out of sight of the house, I began to pick out the terrace and the path down the cliff to a swimming pool and private harbor at the bottom.

A manservant in the Perelada livery showed me through the house and out on to the terrace, where Carmen sat at a table under an umbrella. She didn't appear to be doing anything. After kissing me on both cheeks and pressing a cold Coke into my hand, she asked what I'd like to do. "What do you like to do when you're here?" I asked, speaking English. Her English was as good as my Spanish, so we switched back and forth, depending on our mood.

"My favorite thing," she said, "is to take the boat out and drive to a beach where you can't arrive by land. There are pools—what are they called, those pools where the plants grow? Ah yes: tide pools. There are many tide pools there. And then I like to fish for octopus from the boat on the way back."

"Sounds great to me," I said. "Let's do it."

After she picked up some lunch from the kitchen, she showed me to the changing rooms by the pool, and we set off in the motorboat both wearing bikinis, with a couple of towels and shirts in case the sun got too hot. I have no recollection of what we talked about: the beauty of the coast, perhaps, which at that time was still unspoiled, although further south, where the hills became softer and covered with pine trees, cheap hotels already scarred the landscape; or maybe the fish—red mullet, perch, and little sardines, which we watched from the boat as they swam among the rocks and weed, all clearly visible to the bottom. For a while we, too, swam around, breathing through snorkels and making faces at each other through our masks, while the anchored boat rocked very slightly on the lake-calm sea. All day long there were caresses that rarely involved physical touch, but which passed softly from one to the other through our eyes. Just once, we put suntan lotion on each other's back, rubbing slowly in absolute silence, both paying the most acute attention to the ever-changing place where fingertips touched skin.

When I left the villa, sunburnt and sad, Carmen kissed me on both cheeks and said, You must come again. But I never did. She never invited me again and I never speculated about why.

A couple of weeks later, a young man from Perelada named Francisco, who pursued me ardently throughout my three years there, took me out on a Sunday afternoon. "I know a beach very quiet. Pretty place too," he said, from which I deduced he knew somewhere he could make out with me in private. As he directed me to his beach, I realized we were heading straight for Garbet, and, indeed, when we came in sight of the villa, he proudly told me that it belonged to "the

Family." "Yes I know," I said, rather abruptly, deciding not to tell him I had spent the day there with Carmen. Such contrasts were hard for all of us in the village, and I didn't need to emphasize my remoteness from Francisco, already being almost a foot taller than he, as well as literate, middle class, foreign, and financially independent. So there, behind a massive rock shaped like a lying-down dachshund, we embarked on a marathon session of back-rubbing (my back, his rub) interspersed with a bit of kissing and groping.

Nobody knew the whole story of my sleeping around. Many people knew one or two threads of it: the boys in Figueras knew and disapproved of Andrés; Señor Dominguez knew about my "boyfriend" Ricardo, who was stationed at the military camp; the night porter at my hotel knew about the Fruco salesmen, Hyacinto and Xavier, both of whom had sneaked upstairs with me on occasions, and pretty much everyone knew about the American boys, the waiter from Rosas, and various other dancing partners who drove in my open car through Perelada or Figueras in the early hours of the morning. I wasn't particularly worried about my reputation, though I probably should have been. Somehow, my lack of concern helped legitimize my extremely unorthodox behavior and encouraged the gossips to regard me with some indulgence, since I merely laughed when they reported having seen me with someone or other in my car the night before. Had I looked guilty, I would have been crucified.

The men weren't important enough to feel guilty about. Mostly I didn't care about them, or if I did, it was a feeling quite separate from the sex. Francisco, for example, became a friend, referring to himself as my "little brother," but those feelings seemed pallid compared with the intensity of the brief emotional connection with Carmen or the secret yearning I carried around for Sophia.

In fact, I had no guilt to spare. It was all absorbed with the terrifying possibility that I might be a lesbian (though I didn't think the actual word). Underneath that was buried the tormenting pictures of Atlantic swells that seethed in the background of my nightly dreams.

WOMEN went in and out of church all day long. From my window, or from a sidewalk opposite the big church on the market square, I watched them, their heads covered with lace or a black scarf, as they climbed the steps to the immense wooden doors. They sidled in looking almost furtive, as if giving in to a great desire for something that waited for them inside there, where the darkness smelled of candles and incense. I envied them their passion and, once or twice, when I dared, I slipped in behind them and gazed up at the soaring vault under which they knelt. I hardly dared look at the gaunt body of the statue whose eyes rolled up white and resigned from the head that lolled to one side, resting on prominent ribs. It all seemed too much: too glorious and too awful to contemplate.

I was fascinated by the banks of candles sputtering in the holy air, and could almost see the great lover waiting back there in the darkness. There was a potent thrill, a fear of discovery, which I recognized from my secret life with Sophia. But what I recognized most, as I watched those women approach the church and slide through the brass-studded door, was their shame—the way their bodies shrank into the black folds of their clothes as if to say I'm sorry, as if to say I'm full of unseemly passions, as if to say, as I, myself, would say through the years to come: I am unworthy, I am nothing, and finally, in the seductive light of a thousand candles: I am yours.

Heavy-limbed from too much alcohol, I sometimes spent the long, hot afternoons at Perelada in the cloister by the chapel. Father Luís spent his afternoons there too, dozing on a stone bench, his hands clasped in the lap of his cassock, his sandaled feet planted squarely on the inscribed flagstones, which were worn into soft hollows by centuries of feet. Gradually his chin would drop to his chest until his bass snores accompanied the chorus of cicadas. In front of him, graceful arches opened on to a small, square garden, surrounded on four sides by the shaded cloister. In the center, a fountain trickled steadily into a stone basin and spilled over into a profusion of creeping ivy, from which the lizards emerged to sun themselves on rocks. The priest, motionless in his corner, slept in the shadow of the chipped stone sarcophagus which hung on the wall above his head.

I would stare at the fountain until it mesmerized me. When I achieved a kind of stupor, induced by the rhythmic sounds of sleep and cicadas, of water and my own breathing, and by the heat that wrapped itself closer and tighter as the afternoon trundled towards evening, I could almost see the ghosts of the Carmelites floating in and out of the chapel. If I stayed there long enough, I could long for their reclusive life.

Other times I went into the chapel and sat in a pew to stare up at the carved ceiling. I liked feeling small and self-important at the same time and being overwhelmed by something that, for once, wasn't sex or falling in love, but which functioned as effectively as either one of those to blot out my mother approaching the ladder that dropped to the black swells of the Atlantic.

It was envy of the comfort the women seemed to find in their churches that finally motivated me to approach Father Luís. When, one afternoon, I sat down on the bench beside him, he was eager to talk. Up close, he lost the aura of competence bestowed by the black cassock. His face showed the broken veins of a drinker and his breath smelled of onions. As usual, my conversational gambits were limited by my discomfort with the language and he, too, suffered from the switch from Catalan to Spanish. Perhaps this accounts for our very different interpretations of my first, shy question: "Will you tell me about the Catholic Church, Father?"

Far from recognizing my young, searching soul—far from embarking on a theological discussion that would address sin, death, the afterlife, and the comforting daily presence of a loving God, Father Luís explained instead how his parish fitted into the larger scheme of things. Garriguella, a village about the same size as Perelada, five miles down the road to the sea, had, he told me, more than its fair share of the available Catholic wealth. Linked bureaucratically, first to the nearby Figueras, and then to Gerona, the provincial capital, Perelada had to play its political cards right to get what Father Luís thought was its due. Apparently, Father Tomás at Garriguella—whose name Father Luís spat out with disdain—was more adept at the game.

My memory of that conversation is of a man physically transforming in front of me: the sort of metamorphosis you see in horror movies, where a kindly old man sprouts fangs, while his eyes turn red and start to flash. In fact, he just leaned forward, resting his elbows on his spread knees while I listened reluctantly as if to a smutty secret confided by a stranger.

* * *

IN spite of my intense feelings for Sophia, I had fallen in love with another woman during the winter in England. Now I took long weekends off work and drove back to Dieppe, catching the overnight ferry to Newhaven. But staying up all night for three days in a row—two on the road and one with Josie—soon took its toll. I was getting too tired to sustain the relationships I was hooked on. Nor was sex with men any longer an adequate distraction; I only went on doing it to keep up heterosexual appearances, and out of habit. With women, I needed more and more intensity. Later, I got involved with someone else, while still in love with Josie, having no idea why I did it. Naturally, my inability to explain my erratic behavior compounded the guilt. Meanwhile, I had become an expert at intrigue.

It wasn't until my last summer in Figueras that I began to learn how to create periods of rest in this chaotic life—a lesson I surely learned for survival. That was the summer I discovered the rock in the river near Pont de Molins and began spending time alone there. It was a flat rock right in the middle of a fast-flowing river and I found it by accident one day, driving up a dirt road looking for a remote restaurant someone had told me about. I never found the restaurant, but I returned over and over to the river, sometimes taking afternoons off work with fabricated excuses, just to go and lie there like a stranded fish, with the water roaring around me and the sun burning my spray-soaked skin.

Pretty soon, my desire to go to "my rock" was almost as compelling as my overactive nightlife. The grief I had been avoiding so strenuously was still years away from expression. I didn't think about anything in those blessed intervals. I just lay flat on my back, the rock cold and wet under my shoulders, the sky fierce and blue.

El Cordobés

 DRIVING TO WORK, DRIVING to the beach, then driving to Rosas or Cadaqués again in the evening, I covered a lot of miles, all of them in my open car. On these drives I felt close to the earth, smelling the great gusts of sage which rushed past as I twisted and turned across small bridges over dry streambeds, breathing in the warm salt of the Mediterranean. Approaching a village—Vilajuiga perhaps, or Castello de Ampurias—the smells of earth and sage would be replaced by the smell of cows. I would cross an open sewer, stinking unbelievably in the hot sun, and then slow down as a patchwork of brown stains on the road indicated a cow crossing. Cows lived inside during the heat of the summer, but you could always tell where they were: together with swarms of big flies that bit, their aroma hung over whole villages, over-

whelmed only by the smell of the bakery right after the bread came out of the oven. Then that delicious domestic smell would waft out, along with a steady stream of people carrying loaves under their arms.

But as autumn approached, on those odd days when I had to put the hood up because it rained or was cold and windy, I started to feel cut off from the land. It was claustrophobic inside that small car, only the most pungent cow smells reaching in, and the immense vista across the plain reduced to the view through a narrow windshield and side windows. It was after a couple of rainy days inside this box that I felt the urge to get out of the car and go into the hills on foot. So I asked the guys at work how I could find my way up there.

"¡Ay, Judith!" said Tomás, who teased me mercilessly. "It's much too dangerous. You can't go walking around up there with the snakes and crazies. You might decide to join them, knowing you!"

Some residents of Perelada said the hills were populated with *locos*—people who had wandered off and become crazy hermits. I never heard much evidence for this view, but it served as well as bigfoot myths or ghost stories to keep people from straying too far from home. I wasn't afraid of *locos*, but I was certainly daunted by the prospect of snakes. Growing up in England, I had bypassed the whole notion of danger in the wild. We had no bears, no poisonous snakes except adders, which weren't a patch on rattlesnakes, no wolves or cougars, not even poison oak or poison ivy. The worst danger I had ever encountered was the bed of stinging nettles my pony bucked me into when I was twelve, which was uncomfortable, since I was wearing shorts, but certainly not life-threatening.

Enrique's son looked up from the comic book he was permanently reading, and said disinterestedly, "Why don't you take El Cordobés? You're on such good terms with *los grandes!*"

Los grandes was what the boys in the office called the Mateu family when they wanted to sneer. This time, the sneer was for me and my favored status, but I ignored it. El Cordobés was the name of a popular bullfighter, but I did not see how I could get a bullfighter to go with me on a mountain hike, so I said, "What do you mean?"

"*El caballo,*" the boy said, without looking up. "The horse at *la granja.*"

I turned to Tomás, who nodded. "*Sí, sí.* But it's a very old horse."

That afternoon, having received permission from Carmen to ride the horse, I walked down the long, rutted cart track to the farm, looking for someone called Carlos. The dust had been laid down by two days of rain, and the ground was very slightly softened on the top, though still baked hard underneath. The sky had cleared, the low, grey rain clouds moving away to the north, although a few still hung around the higher mountaintops. Cheerful white clumps of cumulus thinned out across the brilliant blue, making way for the sun and, as the ground dried under the hot rays, the pervasive smell of warming earth rose all around me.

At the end of the track I came upon a cluster of barns and sheds, several trucks jacked up in various stages of dismantlement, and chickens all over the place, pecking at the ground. María's husband, whose name I had forgotten, was leaning headfirst into the engine of a truck, banging around in that vague way mechanics do when they seem to know nothing about what's wrong.

"*¡Hola!*" I shouted, and he emerged, grease all over his face.

Since we had been introduced before, he took a rag and carefully wiped his right hand. I shook it. "Is Carlos around?"

The mechanic gestured towards the back of the barn. "He's over there, mending harness. You'll find him."

After pausing for a minute to wonder what *guarniciones* meant, I entered the cool darkness of the barn and guessed "harness" only after I saw Carlos sitting on a bale of straw, working with a needle and thread on a mule trace. He was an old man, or seemed that way to me, though he might have been only fifty, with a grey beard and a slow, patient manner. Just the kind of man who belonged with animals. When I asked about El Cordobés, his eyes lit up. "You know how to ride, *señorita?*"

When I told him I had owned a horse for many years, he took my arm and led me to the stable, which was a partitioned corner of the barn. There I met El Cordobés, a magnificent creature with the dished nose of an Arab and the strong body of a quarter horse.

"He used to be with the Spanish Riding School of Vienna," Carlos told me, with justifiable pride. I had seen the magnificent Lipizzaner stallions after pleading with my mother to make an excursion to their show in London for my tenth birthday.

"Was he trained to *haute école* like them?" I said, hardly able to connect the spectacular shows I had seen at the Harringay Stadium with this sweet horse nuzzling my arm and nudging me for a treat.

"*Si, señorita,* he was trained in that tradition, but his color never matched any of the teams."

I peered over the stable door, apologizing to El Cordobés for my lack of treats and stroking his neck. He was a bay with three white socks and a wide blaze down his face.

"So how did he end up here?"

"Well," said Carlos, speaking carefully so I would understand, "he was sold to a family, which entered him in international dressage contests. At fifteen, they thought him too old to continue, so they sold him on to someone in the Mateu family who liked riding for just a few months but then abandoned the horse."

El Cordobés nibbled my arm with his long top lip. "Doesn't anyone ride him now?" I asked.

"*No, señorita.* I used to ride him, but my back has grown too stiff for me to ride now. The horse grazes outside in the winter and spring and comes into the barn when the sun begins to be hot."

El Cordobés was well groomed, in spite of his inactivity. His swayed back and something about his eyes betrayed his age, which Carlos said was about twenty-five, but otherwise he looked quite sprightly. So I made a plan with Carlos to go out on the horse as soon as I had a free afternoon, and we shook hands on it.

I HAD never been very long without a horse in my life. The first was Tammy, short for Tamerisk, a bright bay New Forest pony I had fallen in love with when I was seven or eight and learning to ride at Mrs. Tracey's riding school in Brighton. The most treasured present of my first decade had been a small, oval brooch with his head carefully painted on it by a woman who specialized in such portraits. When I fell off my bicycle, breaking two bones in my arm, the brooch hit the gravel first and Tammy was scraped from its polished wood surface. My tears at the hospital were not, as my mother thought, for the pain of my injuries, but rather for the ruin of my favorite possession.

At Mrs. Tracey's I learned a lot about life. Mucking out, cleaning tack, grooming and feeding the horses, I rubbed shoulders with other horse-crazy kids, many of them teenagers and all of them girls. Although I never made friends with any of them (the horses were much more appealing), I listened carefully to their complicated intrigues and their opinions on fashion and music, as well as the intricate gossip of the show-jumping scene, always alert to new, forbidden knowledge. I was also on the lookout for free rides, which I earned by spending long hours at the stables, helping out.

On the Saturday afternoon following my conversation with Carlos, the dependable heat had returned, the sky was empty of clouds, and El Cordobés seemed delighted to put on his tack and stroll out of the barn behind me. He stood like a statue while I put my foot in the unfamiliar, ornate stirrup, enclosed over the toe of my boot, and swung myself up into the saddle. The leather reins were stiff from lack of use, but clean. The long curb bit, which I had looked at dubiously, concerned about the horse's mouth, but which Carlos had convinced me was what El Cordobés had been trained to, shone from a recent polishing. Amazingly, the horse had not moved a muscle while I carried out this inspection—quite unlike Magic, the beloved black pony of my teenage years, who used to dance around while I prepared to get on, marching off while I struggled to catch the stirrup with my right foot, and likely as not shying sideways at some imaginary shadow before I gathered up the reins.

Walking El Cordobés down the track towards the village, I realized that I was sitting on an extremely sophisticated animal. His first movement had come only when I shifted my weight in the saddle, prior to setting off. He had moved sideways. When I applied my calves to his sides, he moved in a direction that reflected the relative pressure of each leg. He had a complicated array of directions in which he could move; not just forward, backward, and a left or right turn. He understood diagonals, and fractions of diagonals, so my right leg pressing a little harder than my left would send him off on a path that was a little to the left of straight ahead.

Then there were the reins. I had always been told I had "good hands," which in riding terms means you have a sensitive connection with the horse's mouth, but El Cordobés could feel when I even thought about moving my little finger. His neck would pull in or straighten out; his nose would poke a little or tilt to one side; his head would lift higher or drop. I started to wonder if the movement of his ears back and forth, sometimes together, sometimes separately, was also a result of some muscle twitch on my part of which I was unaware.

All this was very complicated, but quite safe. The horse was never going to do anything he didn't believe I had initiated. After a few minutes I began to enjoy it. I had competed in a few dressage contests several years earlier, though Magic had been uncooperative to say the least, particularly when asked to change legs in the middle of a figure eight. But I had persevered, learned a lot about balance and impulsion, and even won a ribbon or two. So I started playing with El Cordobés. Gradually I discovered his range of paces, which included a smooth jog and a high-stepping trot, a canter I could slow down till he was rocking on the spot, and a moderately fast canter that never really extended into a gallop. I didn't mind this, since there was no suitable terrain for fast movement, and I didn't want him to stumble or hurt his legs. He let me back him up and he would pivot around both his front legs and his rear ones. He also did a perfect half-pass and, if I managed to shift my weight appropriately and touch the correct rein just enough to suggest it, he would execute a flying change of the leading leg while cantering in a straight line.

It felt very familiar, being alone with a horse. El Cordobés kept his brown ears pricked just as Magic had pricked his black ones up on the ridge of the downs, and occasionally cleared his nose with that friendly snorting-out sound, which is so unlike a snort that it really should have its own name. The scent of his horse sweat rose around me—that smell my mother used to complain about so frequently when I came to dinner, my jeans still caked with the pungent dander.

"You smell like a stable," she used to say sternly, knowing that I took her observation as a compliment.

When finally the decision had been made to get me a horse of my own, my mother enlisted my "horsey" Aunt Joan in the search, and the three of us drove down to Wiltshire, where a friend of Joan's had a reliable, fourteen-two-hand pony for sale. He was only four years old then, and inclined to spook at candy wrappers and sudden birds, but Aunt Joan rode him round the paddock and popped him over a couple of small jumps, proclaiming him suitable, which freed me up to fall in love with him on the spot. My mother had been my champion in that enterprise, standing up to my father's objections and, I suspect, providing the money from her own savings. My father was more than a little afraid of horses: "Dangerous at both ends," he used to say, showing little interest in my occasional triumphs at the Pony Club.

On bitter winter days when I was in school till well after dark, my mother would go to the farm where Magic was boarded and feed him a hot bran mash. This involved entering the twelve-acre field that Magic shared with some ten other horses and finding a way to make sure that he, and he alone, ate the mash, in spite of the hungry herd kicking and biting to get at the bucket. Valiantly, my mother braved them—I know this because I arrived one day to see her shouting and waving her arms furiously at a particularly nasty chestnut gelding who had his ears laid back flat to his head and his yellow teeth lunging at my mother. "Go away, you brute," my mother snarled, sliding the bucket out to the side where Magic hovered, obviously accustomed to this trick.

Summers too, she had given up whole days to come and support me at the local shows I entered. She had been there on that late August day when I had the accident at the gymkhana at a farm near the Devil's Dyke. Sitting in the car at the ringside, and probably reading a book when I wasn't looking, she witnessed the "Gretna Green race" I entered with my friend Leila whose pony, Coral, was suitably small and fast. Once around the ring at a gallop, Leila was leading the pack when I vaulted on over Coral's tail, a move we had practiced for weeks, and we took off together to win the race. Unable to stop, however, we left not only the ring, but the whole showground. When finally we galloped back and stopped dead, in front of the judges' enclosure, I flew through the air and landed on the concrete-hard, chalky ground, shoulder first. The nice Red Cross lady rushed out of her tent and hoisted my arm into the air. "Not broken," she declared. "Right as rain tomorrow." But tomorrow it was not right as rain and I ended up, not for the first time, in the hospital and a plaster cast, my mother sitting at my side.

For years I hoped my mother would acquire a soft spot for Magic. She certainly tried—and was tested quite severely when I took to riding into town and tying Magic to our back gate while I ate lunch. Day after day, he cleverly picked the knot with his teeth and wandered up the back path, where he would stick his head and sometimes his whole front half through the door into my mother's kitchen. She would turn from her lunch at the kitchen table, or drop a plate into the sink, and exclaim, "Now what are you doing in here, you naughty thing!" I chose to ignore the start of fear in her eyes as she reached out a hand towards him.

THE second time I went out on El Cordobés, I had checked out the lie of the land and decided we would go further afield. He twitched an ear with surprise when I picked a path he didn't expect, but followed my directions as always. This time we gained more altitude and the hills stretched out all the way to the glittering sea in front of us. Goats scurried off behind big rocks when we startled them on the path, and, although El Cordobés was a companionable presence, I felt alone with my thoughts and with the calming colors of the landscape. The horse made it easy for me be alone—but not too alone. I smelled the sweat rising from his neck, hummed along with the cicadas, and swayed and daydreamed to the rhythm of his walk.

One Sunday morning when I was nine or ten, before I acquired Magic, I biked over to Mrs. Tracey's. The horses were not all booked and Mrs. Tracey needed something picked up from a farm across the Waterhall golf course, so of course I volunteered to ride over there. Sally, an older girl, offered to accompany me, and we set off, she on a small mare, and I on a lanky old grey called Carnival. I had only ridden Carnival a few times before, always a bit intimidated by his height and the bony neck and withers that swayed at his ungainly trot, and lurched with his canter. He'd been coughing a bit that morning, so Mrs. Tracey said to take it easy.

We jogged down the road, iron shoes ringing out on the black tarmac, sitting up straight in our hacking jackets and black caps and raising our whips to the few people who shouted good morning as they took in their milk bottles or picked their runner beans for lunch. When we turned off onto the narrow path that climbed the side of the downs, Carnival began to wheeze. He put his head down and cleared his nose a couple of times as the path grew steeper and the barbed wire fence on our right gave way to the neatly trimmed hedge that marked the border of the golf course. A few elderly men, colorful in their Aertex shirts, trudged towards the ninth hole with golf bags slung over their shoulders.

All of a sudden, without warning, Carnival's knees buckled and he tilted forward. Still seated, I assumed he was trying to get down and roll, which several of the ponies I knew were in the habit of doing. I slapped him sharply with my whip on his hindquarters and said sternly, "Geddup, giddiup," using my heels and my voice to take charge. But he simply stayed still, kneeling on the path as if in prayer, and wheezing until the wheeze turned into a cough and his nose dropped to the ground. When I sensed he was about to go all the way down, I hastily slid off. Slowly his back end subsided as he rolled to the left. I went forward to his head and bent down. The horse was coughing a dry cough, his eyes staring wildly as he made a couple of feeble attempts to raise himself on to his front legs, falling back each time until the third time he sank down even further, his head falling into the grass.

I didn't want to see what was about to happen.

"I'll go and get help," I said, my voice shrill with panic.

Whatever was going on felt way too big for me to deal with. I was jumping nervously from foot to foot. "I'll go really fast. They'll be here in no time, don't worry."

I grabbed the mare's reins and swung up into the saddle as Sally said "Go quickly, but be careful on the steep parts."

I have no doubt that I went fast. Afterwards, I pictured it as something like the journey my English teacher made us read about in "How They Brought the Good News from Ghent to Aix." Yes, surely I, too, galloped and galloped. Swerved around gorse bushes. Hopped over ditches, urging the mare on with a squeeze of my calves and a constant anxious clucking until she became that heroic "stout galloper," Roland, the only one of the three horses to survive the grueling dash to Aix. Finally, I turned on to the road, hoofs ringing out the triple beats of a horse cantering on asphalt, a horse with a mission, a horse bringing bad news.

I have a vague memory of one of the teenagers, the one who was Carnival's "special" girl, standing in a clean bed of straw in his loose box and crying. I suppose that must have been after the news came back that the horse had died up there by the golf course, but I'm pretty sure no one told me directly. For a long time, I assumed this was because they thought it was my fault. Perhaps they believed I had made him canter up the hill, though surely Sally would have borne witness to our sedate pace. My mother, when she came, was unusually solicitous, helping me gather my belongings and opening the car door for me. On the drive home, she chatted brightly about what we would have for lunch and our plans for the rest of the day.

I remember with the clarity of a well-learned lesson that she never mentioned what had happened that morning, and I remember, too, the feelings that took over my body on that short car ride: the ache in an unidentifiable spot inside my ribs; the tightness in my arms as I hugged them around my chest. Ten years later, frozen with that same strange ache, I hadn't yet unlearned what my mother taught me so well that day: in the presence of death, it's best to change the subject.

I PUSHED El Cordobés into a slow jog as the stony path gave way to crisp grass. Then, reining him in, I rested one hand on his neck and let him pick his own way down the track towards Perelada as I breathed in the mellow warmth of late afternoon, aware only of the sound of hoofs striking stones, and the ever-present tang of salt on the breeze.

When I was a teenager, being alone with Magic had saved my sanity; he and I roamed the Sussex Downs even after most of my friends moved on from horses to boys. Socially incompetent, too tall, and slow to develop, I dissipated my shame up there on Magic, listening to his breath as we trotted among the gorse bushes, and whooping as we galloped flat out along the skyline. I learned, during those difficult years, how to put my human inadequacies in perspective in the rush of a hot wind and the vastness of an empty sky.

Sometimes, now, when I am in the city and life seems too frantic, I open a window and just breathe to calm myself. It's not that the air is clean, any more than the smooth green water of the Mediterranean was clean, but it feels fresh and clear like that water. It's not that I can smell sagebrush or ocean; all I smell is damp compost and the smoke from woodstoves. But it works because the air is part of the sky, part of the trees, part of the grass—because it's out there touching clouds and the warm skins of animals I can't see.

The Rain in Spain

 BY LATE SUMMER THE HILLS were dry, every rock and piece of dirt was dry, the stream beds, river beds, hollows in the ground that might have been dew ponds were all dry. The air was dry as you breathed it into your lungs. The needles that lay under the parched pines were brittle. But the lizards, cacti, and a host of succulents, which had flowered exquisitely in spring when the rain was more generous, flourished in the desert of high summer.

The only water in sight was the blue ocean, almost always visible in the distance, gleaming between two bare shoulders of rock, or lying at the bottom of a distant bay, slick as oil in the midday sun. The only water, that is, except for the occasional flash flood that came pouring down the complex network of ditches after a storm in the mountains, gathering size and momentum as the small waterways converged into one riverbed and ultimately raged in a torrent through some village, where it would pick up a few cars from the *riera* and dump them into the sea.

This happened regularly at certain towns south of Figueras. Caldetas, haunt of my teenage years, together with its neighbor, Arenys de Mar, were two such towns. Back then, shoppers strolled along the *riera,* which, in spite of being a riverbed, was a regular street lined with stores. Nobody seemed to worry that a wave would suddenly appear, curling its crest like an ocean breaker, to snatch the housewives and their parcels up like shells and dump them with the flotsam at the tideline. Floods were just a fact of life, and the residents knew better than to park their cars in the *riera* when it was raining up in the hills. It was always tourists who lost their Citroëns and Volkswagens.

In the fifties, my Aunt Joan joined my parents and me on one of our holidays in Caldetas. Joan had long been my favorite relative, not only because of her crucial role in bringing Magic into my life but also because she was a real artist. Particularly well known as a painter of horses and dogs, she was often commissioned to do portraits of the winners of big races, but the walls of her house, and a few large galleries too, bore witness to her skill with landscape and still life in both oils and watercolor. I visited her at least once a year, drawn back by the smells of linseed oil and gin that permeated her studio and her person, and by the absentminded but joyful distraction she displayed when she was working on a canvas.

In Caldetas, she set off every morning with a rucksack full of supplies and set up her three-legged stool right in the middle of the *riera.* Since she refused to make concessions to the climate and abandon her year-round outfit of tweed skirt, starched cotton shirt and sensible shoes, she was more than a little conspicuous, and soon attracted a crowd of twenty or thirty little boys. After they got tired of pointing and dancing around her as if she were some totemic object, they took to creeping up behind her and trying to touch her paints or the canvas. Since they never left her for a minute during the several hours she spent there, she conversed with them in sign language but was always looking for ways to keep them at bay so she could actually see what she was painting.

One morning she summoned up all her dramatic talent and the few Spanish words she knew. Pointing up the *riera* with a look of great alarm on her face, she shouted, "*¡El agua viene, el agua viene!*" "The water's coming!" and all the boys ran screaming up the side streets. Of course they were soon back, but her trick caused much merriment and was repeated by the children every few minutes for the next two weeks, never failing to scatter them in all directions, during which time Aunt Joan managed to get a good look at the bridge or the tree or the horse dozing in the shafts of its cart.

In Perelada, people sighed for a drop of rain—but not I; I groaned when the sky got overcast. Bad weather meant two things: first, I would be frantically busy at work because all the tourists would abandon the beach and look for interesting local excursions, which put the Perelada winery right at the top of the list; and, second, I would be deprived of swimming. Rain was all very well, but it wasn't the kind of water you could wrap yourself in, like the ocean.

When it did rain, a few heavy drops fell slowly from the sky, several feet apart, as if to tantalize the rain lovers with a sample of what was stored up in the thick clouds. More often than not those clouds moved on without unloading the deluge that bulged in their bellies. The ration of drops allocated to us just went on hitting the ground with a series of thuds, leaving their individual prints in the dust until everything, as far as you could see, was pockmarked. Then it would stop. As the clouds slowly retreated over the mountains, they sometimes added a postscript to this message about who, exactly, was in charge, in the form of rumbling thunder or spectacular lightning flashes that knocked out all the power.

One night I was eating dinner alone in the Hotel Paris dining room next to one of the long windows. First, the white gauzy curtain, usually draped elegantly to the black and white tiled floor, started to flap wildly. A cold wind disturbed napkins and tablecloths at the unoccupied tables across the spacious, old-fashioned room, gusting up to the high ceiling and swishing into dim corners filled with aspidistras. After I had run to my room to fetch a sweater, I continued eating asparagus with homemade mayonnaise, and watched the scene on the *rambla* outside. People were converging on the square with even louder exclamations than usual, tilting their faces up and reaching out their hands, palms up. The tall sycamores rustled as heavy drops struck their leaves, and the birds created an awful cacophony.

When the lightning struck, everyone disappeared from the streets fast. I went on eating my *arroz a la cubana*. When the lights went out, a nervous chatter ran round the dining room, but I just put down my knife and fork, being used to this ritual, and waited for the waiters and Señor Fernando to troop in with a pair of candles for each table.

"*¿Y qué postre?*" inquired the waiter, as if nothing unusual were going on. Indeed his question was reassurance itself, since he asked every night what dessert I would like, and the choices were always the same—flan or ice cream. As I ate my flan, I looked out of the window to see if the whole town was in darkness, but there were lights showing on the other side of the *rambla*. Figueras had two circuits and sometimes it was the other side that had to use candles while we, tranquilly and rather smugly, rode out the storm with our lights on.

Such rainstorms were rare in August. Late September or early October was when the weather usually broke, often holding back the rain through a period of intense, overcast humidity, during which nerves became frayed, cars got driven off bridges into riverbeds, and donkeys brayed petulantly, while the flies tormented them in one last frenzy of summer. But the weather had broken early this year, bringing busload after busload of tourists to the winery as the cold wind drove all those sunburnt bodies from the beach. I would have sympathized with the grouchiness most of them displayed if I hadn't been under so much pressure, sorting them into manageable groups and lining them up at the parking lot.

Where once I'd enjoyed playing the expert with these visitors, I now dragged my feet wearily as I led the way down the stone steps to the cellars. A musky, acidic odor hit my nostrils when I penetrated the solid block of cold air that began at ground level and crept up my legs with each step down. I gestured mechanically towards the various bins, pointing out a special reserve and the hole left in a stack of green bottles where one had exploded. When someone asked about it, I explained, with barely concealed impatience, Perelada's fermentation process. Then I handed out leaflets, pocketed tips, and sent them off for their free tasting, glad to see the back of them.

Sometimes, when it got too crazy, I gave up and sat down

in the bar with a group of visitors and a bottle of champagne, letting the incoming groups swelter in their buses, while the drivers wandered around looking for me. Since they had nothing better to do in this weather, most of the tourists were happy to stay at the bar and get drunk, at which point I would wearily get to my feet and gather up the next tour, leaving Rosé and María to push the sodden drinkers back on to their buses.

Several times, I went back to Figueras after a day of chaos, wanting nothing better than to climb into my bed, put my head underneath something, and stay there until it was reliably summer again. My depression was out of all proportion to the brief change of weather; after all, it might take a week to brew up to the storm, but after that, the sun would shine again and I could, if I chose, keep on swimming right through September and October.

My job, so enviable when I described it to the holidaymakers I met at fashionable nightspots, became a demanding daily routine: I got tired from hard work instead of hard play. Reckless drives late at night lost their romance when they took place under a heavy, overcast sky instead of a million stars. Even the good-natured banter of my friends at the café on the *rambla* turned sour, as good humor gave way to semi-serious bickering, and all of it seemed utterly superficial anyway. I had managed not to think about my parents' deaths by starring in my own summer show. But now the blue backdrop had been pulled out from behind the carefully constructed stage set, and I was out there in the footlights, in danger of having to acknowledge how alone I was.

One grey day late in September, the clouds hung off the Pyrenees for the sixth day in a row and thunder growled through the dense heat. Wearily, I helped an old Belgian woman up the steps of her tour bus, joking with her about how much champagne she had drunk. She blushed with guilty pleasure as I handed her the two bottles she had bought to take with her, wrapped in their corrugated cardboard skins. I breathed a sigh of relief as I waved the bus out of the parking lot. It was almost 8:30, Las Cavas was closing up for the night, and not even the most ardent sightseer could expect anything from me at this hour.

I threw myself down in a chair outside the bar to finish my last glass of *semi-sec* before heading back to town for dinner. I was slightly nauseous from all the alcohol, and the smell of cows seemed more pungent at that moment than it ever had. Swarms of flies hung overhead—not the big, black flies that buzz loudly and swagger on to your skin, but brown, soft-spoken flies that I've only ever seen around farmyards. I smoked a cigarette to keep them away.

Just then the sky was lit up by a flash that seemed to split the firmament in two. For a second a giant crack appeared, as if the grim façade of the all-powerful rain god had been ripped apart. I felt a surge of excitement and fear. What if the sky did open up and let go?

There was a clatter of glasses from the bar as Rosé and María hurried to clean up and get home. Lightning flashed on and off like a lightbulb making intermittent contact. Maybe this time it was really going to give it to us! The raindrops got faster and faster, quickly drenching my hair, but I couldn't move. Terrified of I don't know what, I gripped the arms of the chair.

María stuck her head round the door:

"Come inside, Judith," she said.

"In a minute," I replied. "You go on home now." And she banged the door shut.

Soon I was sitting in a torrent of water. My shirt was soaked and sticking to my body. My feet, in sandals, were submerged in a pool that gathered under my table and chair. The crashes of thunder were so loud it seemed miraculous that things didn't fly apart, shattered by the sound. Water pouring down my neck reminded me of tears, yet if I was crying I would never have known it since my own meager drips would surely have been lost in the midst of that great flood from above. Alone there at the center of the storm, I felt a surge of relief as if something that had been clenched tight for three years had finally grown too tired to hold on. I threw my head back, letting the rain beat on my face, and started to yell with the thunder.

I stayed out there watching the sky until the last rumble died away and nothing could be heard except the mad rush of rivulets searching out new, more effective, escape routes.

PART TWO

Making Waves

I WAS SETTLED INTO A LIFE IN Oregon when I thought one day about my father's home movies, many of which had been made during our Caldetas holidays in the fifties. Eager to revive those old images, and perhaps some of the memories they contained, I tracked down two reels which had been stored in my nephew's attic in England and brought them back to Portland. I took them to be transferred onto video and, soon after picking up the two cassettes, set aside a long, quiet afternoon in which to revisit the past. As I sat on the couch, Oregon rain wandering down the windowpane, memories did begin to flood back, not of the Spanish vacations, but of the filmmaking itself: an activity permeated with that blend of delight and horror that marks the ritual undertakings of most families.

I leaned back into the cushions on the couch, aware of the muted tapping of the raindrops, and remembered the sound tracks. Ah—those sound effects! Waves breaking on beaches; yellow taxis honking and squealing round the plaza; birds, horses' hoofs, ascending jet planes, screaming children, applause.... We had them all on the special records that my father bought from a catalogue, and what we didn't have we improvised using the "Helpful Hints" column in his monthly photography magazine. Back then, the magazine had gone in for photos of happy families sitting in front of their newly installed picture windows, engaged in the congenial family activity of putting sound effects onto their home movies. Sometimes the mother was coming in through the door in a crisp cotton dress with a plate of cookies, while the father and children looked up from their spools and records and coconut-shell horses' hoofs, with smiles of sincere appreciation. My father, it seemed, thought we were one of these families.

My parents and I would watch the film on the silvered screen when it first came back from being processed. It clicked noisily through its obstacle course of gates and tunnels on the bright red projector.

"You can't see properly if you sit on the side like that, dear," my father said every time, prior to explaining at great length how the beaded screen only reflected the image directly forward.

"Don't worry, dear. I can see fine," my mother would reply, perched on the arm of a chair, poised to leave if the phone rang or her bakewell tarts got done.

After this first viewing and some editing, the film was sent off to have the sound strip added, returning a week or two later to be threaded up again, not only through the projector's maze of pathways, but also through the sound head and various sprockets of the recorder.

But these cassettes I now held had no sound tracks. Since the movies hadn't been Super 8 but rather the older eight millimeter films with added magnetic sound strips, it was difficult to transfer the sound. The man who had done the job for me hadn't had the necessary equipment. I considered the missing sound tracks and briefly thought about taking the films to another studio, but rejected the idea. Why would I need the sound when I could supply it with perfect accuracy out of my head? I could even improve on it. There was that place, for example, where the traffic noises ran over into the beginning of the beach scene: Mother and I and the Kings sitting under striped umbrellas, eating melon. I still remembered a particularly indignant car horn cut short mid-honk, as my father yanked the needle off the traffic record and I started tilting the Crawfords Cream Cracker tin full of gravel. (We all thought this tin made better waves than the "beach sounds" record, which had sea gulls mewing all over it and which sounded more like Cornwall than the Costa Brava.) No, I didn't want to listen to that mistake any more. I would provide my own perfect transition from the Barcelona rush hour to cantaloupe juice and salty skin.

I pulled the first cassette from its box. Neatly printed on the label was the title, "Spanish Playground." When the guy who made the videos had asked for titles, I had been uncertain. Should I play it safe and label them: "Home Movies, Spain, 1959," or should I defer to the memory of my father and come up with some grand cliché like "Spanish Adventure" or "Sun and Sand"? I had decided to use one of his less embarrassing ones.

Titles had been very important to my father. First there were the words of the title, which in his case were nearly always reminiscent of cinema news documentaries of the time. Then there was the visual style—his real obsession. He purchased sets of letters, plastic title holders in frames, and exotic designs to back his titular masterpieces. He sent away for records of fanfares, crashing cymbals, and drum rolls to accompany them and studied the photography magazines for new ideas. Soon he had mastered the technique of superimposing the words of the title on to scenes from the film which, in the case of holiday movies, were usually shots of French roads taken through the windshield from the passenger seat of the car. Long, straight highways unfolded between rows of poplars, leading south to sunshine and Spain, while the camera lurched and jumped, the fanfare trumpeted, and the words of the title appeared. This particular style carried with it the obligation to end the film with a long sequence of the same roads, shot this time out of the back window, preferably with a touch of sunset behind the poplars, as we drove north away from our summer wonderland. The commentary would swell to a grandiose finale: something along the lines of, "And so we leave the hot sun and the bloodstained sand of the Iberian peninsula behind, as we head north into the misty airs of England." And so, too, the words "The End" faded up in front of the receding highway, to the accompaniment of plaintive flamenco music.

To my father, who was an engineer, technique was everything, aesthetic sensibility an unknown concept. Words were not his strong point either. Like many people, he had a few words he continually mispronounced—*negligible* was one, which he always insisted had three, not four, syllables. "The impact was neglible," he would say—and indeed, did say right there on the sound track one day, when reading his commentary onto "Spanish Playground 2."

Usually the titles took only a few hours to shoot, but there was one occasion when the edited film sat around for weeks. He was working on the title, my father explained mysteriously, revealing nothing about his methods. I noticed, however, that he was going down to his basement workshop for a few minutes every morning before he left for the station. Naturally, I went down to have a look. On the workbench he had rigged up an odd contraption: a flat tray lined with sky-blue paper and covered with a jumble of plastic letters, all different colors. Fixed above the tray with various clamps and supports was the movie camera, its lens pointing straight down at the tray. Arranged around it, also directed at the letters, were three floodlights.

Since I couldn't make any sense of this, I waited impatiently for my father's return that night to ask him about it. He seemed annoyed by my questions, but I persisted until he explained that each morning he spent some time moving all the letters a bit and exposing one frame of the film, before moving them a bit more and taking the next shot. The letters, he said, were gradually moving out of their random muddle and would eventually arrange themselves into the words of the title. I begged to make some of the moves, but he refused to allow me near the operation, preferring to take only as many shots as he could fit in before rushing to the station, and I had to wait weeks until he finally sent the title off to be developed.

I had forgotten about it by the time my father invited us to view his new title. My sister and her husband happened to be visiting that weekend and some neighbors had also dropped in, so we gathered ceremoniously in the music room, some of us perched on the grand piano, others leaning against the big old Grundig radiogram or squashed into the bay window seat with the cyclamen plants. The projector hummed and clattered, the lead film flashed on the screen, and then there was the sky-blue background and the letters scurrying around. Bright red *N*'s and *A*'s threaded their way around yellow *O*'s and a purple *S*. For the most part they moved smoothly, though every once in a while one or two of them took a sharp leap, where he had moved them too far, perhaps worried about missing his morning train. Slowly they formulated themselves and lined up until the words appeared in all their glory: "A Panarama of Northern Spain." I was enchanted. This was one of my father's better efforts, I thought, but my mother was noticeably quiet. "Too bad you can't spell panorama," she said at last.

My father lost heart for a while after that, but he bounced back a bit later when he read about dubbing sound to a person speaking on film. Soon he had me settled at the dining room table, spruced up in my school uniform, hair tied back in a neat pony tail. I memorized the introduction I read to the camera—all about Spain and its modernization, the ballet of the bullfight (I balked at this, but my father insisted), and our exact itinerary, including the time taken to cover each leg of the journey. When my memory failed me, I could refer to the large hand-printed copy of my speech held up by my mother beside the camera. At the beginning, as I began to speak, my father insisted that I very deliberately lower my right hand from my chin to the table as a signal; later, when dubbing the speech on to the sound track, I would be able to tell when my mouth was going to start moving. The dubbing session, when it came, turned out just like all the other sound sessions: sometimes I got it wrong; sometimes I got it right; my mother exhorted everyone to patience; and my father told me I was a fool.

When I slammed out of the room saying, "This is stupid," I nursed a burning core of hatred. I would have cried with rage if crying had been allowed in my family; I would have called him names if I had known any. It wasn't just his apparently benign bullying that got to me, it was the injustice of his tyranny. When particularly agitated, he would stand up and sort of shrug his whole body, jingling the change in his pockets with both hands. Then my mother would chime in with her don't be so impatient, dear, and after a while I would stamp out with my this-is-stupid routine. I never understood why he got to be in charge and why my mother humored him—or, at least, that's what she called it; I called it giving in. I can still see the three of us in that room, my father red in the face, my mother's forehead wrinkled and anxious, and myself, a pouting adolescent, anchored by rage and pain to the Parker Knoll wing chair. Always, in this picture, I am holding the biscuit tin full of gravel—making waves and not making waves all at the same time.

My father and I took our antagonisms wherever we went. Going down to Spain through France, it was his driving—and my mother sided with me on that one. "The child's going to be sick if you drive like that," she would say, as I stared greenly out of the back window. Actually, I had grown out of my childhood habit of throwing up every hour on car trips, but the drives down to Caldetas still felt like torture. I was always secretly searching for a way to make my father look stupid, always dying with embarrassment when he spoke to French gas station attendants as if they were deaf or dim-witted, always hoping against hope that my mother would back me up as I displayed my aggression as a stubborn refusal to cooperate.

"But why do we have to go so far," I would complain, wanting to wander around Albi or Perpignan instead of pushing ahead on my father's inexorable schedule.

One year, in pursuit of the perfect suntan, I decided to stay on the beach through the whole three weeks, deaf to my father's insistence that I should accompany him and my mother on an excursion to Barcelona. "I don't want to go to a bullfight," I said with my lower lip protruding, never quite believing in my own resistance. But it worked and I stayed alone in blissful independence, while he went off and shot the famous footage of the matador, El Cordobés, which he later inadvertently re-exposed, superimposing several leaping salmon on to the distant moment of truth. The hysterical laughter with which the whole family greeted this piece of surrealism was, perhaps, one of my father's own moments of truth— or at least I wanted to think so. I nursed his humiliation like a secret treasure, while everyone else appeared to forget.

I WAS excited about the prospect of seeing the tape of Caldetas; having no one to remember with had made the past particularly elusive all these years. I was also intrigued with the second reel, the one that included a Spanish trip my parents had taken without me, their last holiday before their deaths. That summer they had broken with the Caldetas tradition, driving all the way down to Andalusia instead. Germaine went along too, though she grumbled about missing her old haunts. I had refused to go, having better things to do at the age of eighteen. But now, videotape in hand, I wanted to eavesdrop on that vacation I knew almost nothing about.

I had often imagined my parents on the screen in this last movie, talking, smiling, revealing themselves. I wanted the fondness with which everyone else in my family recalled my father to rub off on me—to replace the teenage hostility I had been stuck with all these years. As for my mother, I missed her as we all miss our mothers, dead or alive, and she had been dead long enough that I couldn't really remember what she looked like. Memory is like that. You carry with you just one piece of the person: a hand gesture, a fold of skin on the neck, a particular largeness or a laugh. Even though you can still describe them, it's not the same as being able to conjure up their face in your mind's eye.

But first I wanted to see Caldetas. I slipped the tape into the VCR and turned on the television. It was all there: the long French road scenes, the horrible panning of the camera off to one side as the car rushed past tree trunks and telephone poles; the Hotel Titus viewed from every angle, including the top of the mountain, which my father climbed just to get an "aerial shot," and the park full of people holding hands in circles, dancing *sardanas*. Could do with some sound track here, I thought, remembering the reedy sound of the *sardana* band, and staring at the oddly silent dancers, who pointed their toes in unison and moved neatly to left and right.

Then the film jumped to a shot of Germaine staring out from behind a barred door set into a cliff, pretending to be a prisoner. I remembered this drama that our friends had spontaneously started to act out when my father turned the camera on them. I think he had been meaning to pan out from the hilltop villa to show the village of Caldetas and the sea full of sailboats, but for once he had been forced to shoot some people. The camera lingered on Peggy and Freddy, owners of the villa, pretending to be ghoulish jailers, swung past my mother wringing her hands in mock horror, and ended with a close-up of Germaine pushing her hand through the bars begging for a crust of bread, the back of her other hand pressed dramatically to her forehead, Sarah Bernhardt style. I had no idea then or now what it was all about, and I don't think the actors, all gallantly holding back waves of laughter, did either. It was what happened when we went to Spain; a happening born of my mother's Spanish persona.

The second tape, sedately entitled "Fuengirola '62," had more road scenes—this time some Spanish roads too, as the journey took my parents down through southern Spain towards Gibraltar, though it never took them across the border. I remembered their tale of breaking down in some village and having to sleep in a café while they waited for a spare part, but that wasn't on the film. Instead there were vistas: brown hills covered with olive trees, views across a white village to the blue ocean far below, and lots of ruins. These vistas very quickly made me nauseous as my father had never cured himself of his superfast panning habit. My eyes strained to keep up as the camera swept through a 180-degree survey, but it was too fast to focus on anything and all the trees and churches became a blur.

Gradually I realized that my father, being the cameraman, was not likely to feature in the film. He never had before; why would he so now in this last film, just because I was finally ready to see him? But surely my mother and Germaine would appear?

Close to the end of the tape, there were some scenes of a Roman ruin. The camera wandered across broken walls and fragments of mosaic floor, then backtracked as if it had just noticed the statue it had whisked past a minute before. It was all un-planned: that was my father's style. He peeked through an archway, swung sideways to show a glimpse of Mediterra-nean, and took in a donkey that stood under some palm trees wearing its straw hat. Then he wobbled towards a large rock. The camera insisted. The rock stayed still. Finally the camera tilted, probably as my father took one hand off to gesture as he shouted.

My mother appeared from behind the rock. She was wear-ing her old green and blue dress. I remembered that dress. For a moment she was painfully, ordinarily familiar as she walked towards the camera, her body moving in a way that was so predictable that I felt my own body moving with her. I watched her hands as they pushed vigorously towards me, urging my father and his camera away, her palms flat against the warm, Spanish air. I knew those hands well: dry and clean as hands get after days of ocean and sand; lined and leathery as my mother's hands always grew in summer; large, strong hands, pulling out roots from her dahlia bed, playing the piano ac-companiment to my clarinet piece, or rhythmically brushing my hair as I, a small child, sat on the floor in front of her chair. Awkward and a little stooped, she looked as if her back hurt as she continued to gesture towards the camera and shouted something. The film whirred on. She mouthed: "Stop it! Stop it!" and retreated behind the rock.

The tape clicked to an end and started to rewind, and for a moment the old powerless rage washed over me. I wasn't just infuriated at my domineering father, although that old anger was still there. It was suddenly much, much more. I was an-gry that they had died before I could cope with it—too old to be an orphan, but too young to manage the world alone. I was angry that they had left me before I could properly leave them, before I could reject them, as all children reject their parents and then, in time, come back to them as adults. I was angry that my father had finally proved his utter lack of qualification for being in charge, but only when satisfaction at his failure was forever lost to me—when I could only despair at the fact that 905 people had been saved, while my father failed to save the two who mattered. Finally, I was enraged that my mother, with her lifelong terror of dying at sea, had had to climb down to her death in the middle of the Atlantic.

I clicked the tape on again and watched it run for a few seconds. Then I pushed the pause button on a market scene. Strings of garlic and peppers hung beside beach hats and barrels of snails. Chickens dangled by their necks from the overhead pole of a street vendor's booth, their yellow feet close to the camera, raking the air with splayed toes. Off in the corner, my mother, still in her green and blue dress, reached her hand across towards an old woman who held a large artichoke. I looked at this still life, wondering what they were saying as the camera caught them by chance. I held them there motionless, as the three of us had been held motionless—my parents and I frozen through all these years inside our own still life.

$Stones$

"YOU'VE NEVER SEEN YOUR parents' gravestone, have you?" my partner, Ruth, asked. We were sitting on a small deck overlooking hundreds of yachts in the Brighton Marina, halfway through a vacation in England.

"No," I replied. I had never been back since my sister and I had gone there twenty-two years earlier to arrange for the stone to be made. It had been September and I was almost through working at Perelada for that summer when my sister flew to Barcelona. I picked her up in the little green car that had been our mother's, and we drove together down the coast, swimming, eating paellas, and singing "The Lass of Richmond Hill," and all the other songs we could remember from childhood, while speeding along with the top down. As I remember it, we never once mentioned our parents.

"Don't you sometimes wish they'd been buried somewhere closer?" Ruth asked, as sea gulls swooped down to snatch crumbs from our table.

I stared through the thicket of masts with their ropes flapping against the metal. Closer to where? True, I had occasionally wished they'd been buried in an English churchyard with spreading oaks to shade their stone, and spring daffodils, Bathshebas perhaps, coming back whiter with each passing year—but this would not have been exactly close to our home in Oregon. Still, if they'd been buried in England it would surely have occurred to me, on one of my visits, to go to the graveyard. Their deaths had always been disembodied. They had died out of sight and were buried that way too.

"Do you think it matters where you are buried?" I asked Ruth.

"It matters to the living more than the dead," she said, and I understood that she was encouraging me to go and see the grave. That's when I realized how much I wanted to.

THE following autumn, we settled in for a two-month stay in the village of Salobreña, due south from Granada and some hundred and fifty miles east of Gibraltar. It was utterly beautiful—close to the snow-covered mountains and the beach. Like Perelada, it sat on a conical hill that rose out of a flat, fertile plain. The fields between the foot of the hill on which the village was built and the beach were filled with bright green sugar cane that blew in ever-changing wave patterns like the blue ocean beyond.

We spent a whole day walking up and down the narrow,

cobbled streets, and the steep staircases of brick laid in careful patterns. In dark bars and small bakeries we asked about empty houses and apartments until, before long, the women who hung around in groups on the street, chatting as they sliced their seed potatoes, started to approach us with suggestions. There was a lovely but impractical old house that had once belonged to the parents of one of these women, still completely furnished with their furniture. It had pottery, handmade at the beginning of the century, and a 1925 wedding photo on the bedside table, but no hot water. Eventually, we decided on a newer but charming apartment high on the hill facing the sea. We could lie on our couch and watch the small sailing boats, the fishing trawlers, and the occasional big tanker cut through the water, which was sometimes dark green like a pond, other times ruffled and sparking silver in the shifting winds.

The day we went to Gibraltar, there was nothing tentative about the sun. The drive was depressing, taking us along the once-lovely Costa del Sol now cluttered with high-rise hotels and junky stores, through fancy condo developments and golf courses, and past laundry-festooned shacks, patched with tar paper and cardboard. At Fuengirola we glimpsed the hotel that had featured in my father's last holiday movie. Not far away, gypsies squatted in the dust and dogs scratched their bellies with their hind feet.

It was sweltering in Gibraltar, on that rock that had, for centuries, held so much strategic power—an incongruous little piece of Britain, attached like an ill-fitting artificial limb to the end of Spain. We crawled in a slow line of traffic through the frontier post, guarded by British police who looked ridiculously out of place, and made a circuit of the town full of black-market vendors and souvenir shops. I barely remembered the cemetery from my previous visit but found it easily and parked the car in the shade of a lime tree, hoping the sun would stay behind its canopy of leaves. Picking up a plan from the office, we walked through an open gate into the hush of the biggest graveyard I have ever seen. Tracing the paths with my finger on the map, I led the way past the Catholic and Jewish areas to the Church of England section.

Traffic rumbled in the distance and cicadas sang their querulous songs. We walked slowly, each of us taking one side of the path, reading inscriptions. There were small marble slabs, rectangular stones, and tall, ornate columns, some of them with angels or crosses, bearing overblown praises of the dead. There were simple stones, so old they were chipped and leaned crookedly into the ground, and there were children's graves, their dates spanning a couple of years or just a few months. The sweat started to pour down our backs as we turned corner after corner, commenting at first on what we read, but becoming quiet as our mouths grew parched and the lines of stones continued to stretch away on all sides.

Two hours later, we stumbled back to the office and asked for help. Mr. Sanchez, the pear-shaped manager in a startlingly blue suit, pulled out a pile of old ledgers and ran his finger down columns of spidery script.

"Ah, yes," he said finally. "Barrington...Reginald and Violet. They were moved in 1964 from two temporary graves to one with a marker. That's correct, no?" I nodded, while he took my plan of the cemetery and circled an area. "This is where all the *Lakonia* victims are buried. They will be there too." He looked at me for a moment, pulling on his peppery mustache as if assessing my state of mind, and apparently concluded that too much time had elapsed for condolences to be necessary.

We had, in fact, already found that area, where the names of several British and a few German people had gone on record as having drowned during the *Lakonia* disaster, but we returned to it, shading our heads now with the folded map, a handkerchief, a canvas beach bag—anything we could hold between our eyes and the relentless afternoon sun. Carefully, we checked the stones again, most of which were half buried by grass and weeds—clearly the graves of people whose families, like us, lived far away.

After a while, Mr. Sanchez appeared looking anxious, perhaps having noticed our car still parked under the lime tree. He was sweating profusely in his shiny suit. "Dear, dear," he muttered, checking his plan against the maze of paths that crisscrossed the section. Then he pointed to a large patch of impenetrable brambles. "Could be there," he said. "Could be there."

He wiped his forehead with a handkerchief and looked at me slightly apologetically before staggering back to his office. Ruth and I collapsed onto a bench. I couldn't decide if I was in a terrible rage or just depressed; I seemed to swing from one to the other by the moment. "How could they…," I began, but I knew my anger to be useless. This was certainly nothing like I had imagined, having anticipated some kind of closure— some acknowledgment, perhaps, of the distance I had come from denial. Much of that journey had happened during my years with Ruth, eased along by her willingness to help me get to the heart of the matter, which she now did once again.

"We have to find the grave," she said. "When we know where it is, we could come back another time. Then you'll be able to do what you came here to do."

I felt great relief. I didn't know what I had come here to do, but I was grateful that it didn't have to be a missed opportunity—just stage one of the enterprise. I never would have thought of making the long trip from Salobreña again.

It was then that I noticed a disheveled grave close by. Its stone had broken off completely and was lying in the grass, face down, partly covered by straggly thistles. With sudden confidence I walked over and managed to lift one end. Leaning over, I read the inscription on the grass-stained face.

WE drove back to Salobreña through the dusk, which rapidly turned to a night punctuated by stars and the lights of hotels. The coastal sprawl grew almost pretty as night blotted out the shoddy paint and cracked walls of apartment buildings thrown together to make a quick buck. After stopping for dinner at our favorite restaurant in Málaga, we drove away from the Costa del Sol on the narrow highway that would take us home, finally able to laugh about our dreadful day. It was dark, with only occasional pinpoints of light out to sea on our right and the beams of our headlights sweeping across rock face and cactus as we swayed to the rhythm of the curves.

"Let's go back in a month," said Ruth, and I agreed.

In the weeks that followed, I walked down the hundreds of steps to the café or along the road between the sugar canes to the beach and found myself wondering how it was different to be there where my parents were actually buried, than to think about them at other times in other places. I began writing down some ideas of what I might do and say when we returned to the grave. I remembered how, a year after Ruth's mother had died, we went back for the unveiling of the headstone and in the traditional Jewish way left stones on the grave—not flowers. I started picking up special stones and tucking them into my pockets.

We took long afternoon walks through the village and up into the olive groves, where aqueducts divided field from field. We rode buses up to the highest villages of the Alpujarras and stayed overnight at an inn overlooking the Poqueira Gorge. We thought about Gerald Brenan, who once lived up there, writing *South from Granada* and his books about the Spanish Civil War, and we imagined the Woolfs and Lytton Strachey riding donkeys up the steep tracks to visit him. When we looked out from Capileira across the mysterious sea to where the coast of North Africa was a blur on the horizon, we were reminded of a reference to that view in Virginia Woolf's *The Waves*. We wondered if she had stood right there where we were standing, and who else had stood there too: the Moorish engineers who built the irrigation system? Federico García Lorca, fleeing Franco's soldiers? History no longer seemed remote but something that spanned past and present. And all the while, between conversations and bus rides, long mornings of work on my poems and trips to the market, I thought about the history represented by the grave in Gibraltar.

Every morning, still drowsy, I walked up to the castle that crowned the Salobreña hill, and circled the crumbling parapets to my special place, a small, square room, open to the sky, with part of the wall still standing, and a trellis structure draped with vines shading one half. The floor was mosaic, worn smooth and hollowed into shallow footprints around the doorway, its colors faded to a light terra-cotta, with browns and greens that merged into one extended earth tone. Here I could sit on the floor, across which lizards scurried from time to time, and lean against the wall with nothing overhead. To the north were the mountains, new snow dusting the peaks almost every day now, and to the south, of course, lay the sea.

One morning, as the sun sent sweat trickling down between my breasts, I thought about all the other places that had provided me with whatever this ruined room, so close to the sky, provided. Places of rest and respite, of nurture and renewal, like the rock in the river near Pont de Molins, where I had escaped for afternoons during those hectic Figueras summers, or the place under the pines on the hillside above Perelada, where I had ridden the old horse, El Cordobés. Sometimes it seemed as if it was those places that had saved me, as if my long journey from the fear of grief into grief itself and this new time of contemplation had begun with those stepping stones—one safe haven after another across the rapids.

I leaned back against the warm bricks. What exactly was it I wanted to do at the cemetery? I wasn't sure. All I knew was that I wanted to be finished with all this. Wanted to be able to look back and say I had come through it and made it out the other side.

Not that I would emerge untouched. Like others who have experienced sudden, unexpected loss on a large scale, I would never regain that sense of immunity I'd once had—never again be able to believe that car crashes, plane crashes, fatal food poisonings—any variety of being in the wrong place at the wrong time—happen only in *other* people's lives. Nor would I ever forget that any parting can be the last—that people can leave saying, "See you in two weeks," and never be seen again.

At twenty, I had tried to hide the terrors that accompanied this knowledge, just as I hid what I considered the shameful blot of tragedy, under an energetic cloak of normality. But by forty, I had acknowledged the fears; the knee-jerk panics that had once gripped me when Ruth boarded a plane, or when I had to board one myself, had largely disappeared.

For years I had had to grapple with that fear of flying. Logically, I should have become frightened of ships; everyone thought so. When I decided to go to America for the first time in 1975 and booked passage on the *QE2*, my friends had looked at me with compassion, thinking I was putting myself through some kind of grizzly trial when, in fact, I was simply avoiding the only alternative: a plane. I paid no particular attention to the handsome Cunard captain who steered us across the Atlantic, although when I traveled by plane I always peered anxiously at the pilots in their cockpit, joking and flipping switches as I ducked in under the doorway. Lingering beside the first-class galley, I would try to assess from the backs of their heads and the forearms that protruded from white, rolled-up shirtsleeves, whether or not they were trustworthy, whether or not they had had enough sleep. The *Lakonia* stewards had fought their way into lifeboats ahead of the passengers; the radio operator had huddled under his blanket while a female tourist rowed; and Captain Matheos Zarbis had gone to jail for gross negligence in fighting the fire and evacuating the passengers, and for abandoning his ship. But I only worried about aircraft pilots.

What I had gleaned from my parents' deaths was not that ships are dangerous, but that *what you fear most* is. My mother had been afraid of the sea and it was the sea that snatched her, just as she had predicted.

I knew, too, that I would always coexist uncomfortably with the disasters of strangers. Like anyone else, I scrutinized newspaper accounts of train wrecks and freeway pileups, missing children, and random shootings, but even while I read the details I wanted to strangle the journalists who stuck their cameras and notebooks and microphones into the faces of the hunched figures anxiously waiting for news. I wanted to berate the gawkers, yell at them to go home and mind their own fucking business. I knew that some of those worried people were about to be overwhelmed by unimaginable sorrow and that the journalists, the photographers, the eager voyeurs, and even most of their friends, hadn't a clue about that pain. To them it was a thrill, a horrid, fascinating story they could talk about with each other. *Isn't it dreadful?* they would say, and *Can you imagine?* But I knew they couldn't.

WHEN we made our second trip to the cemetery, the sun was still hot but lacked the antagonism of that first afternoon. Off to the right a construction crew made drilling noises, while somewhere to the left two children ran around, called back to order at regular intervals by their mother's weary voice.

At the graveside it was very still. Ruth stood in the shade of a hibiscus while I sat on a large rock near the headstone, which we had paid Mr. Sanchez to have repaired. Markers fringed with straggly grass and weeds lined up in all directions, but this place between the two paths, a block down from the wide bench-lined avenue, was becoming our neighborhood in the great city that was the cemetery. The brambles loomed off to the right. Our dusty piece of ground was patterned with our footprints.

I placed the special stones I had collected on the grave, and laid a hibiscus flower in the long grass. I had little faith that Mr. Sanchez would keep the brambles from swallowing up the grave, given the twenty-two-year interval that had separated my two visits. Still, I was no longer unhappy that my parents were buried there: I even began to see a kind of rightness about it. I looked down at the ground, hard and white as concrete, and it struck me then that they would have liked to be buried in Spain, where they had spent so many happy years. Technically, of course, this wasn't Spain, it was British soil, but no matter what the map said, the underground layers knew the truth—rock shelves and stubborn earth merging seamlessly with the rest of the great Iberian peninsula. I looked north through the heat haze towards the hills—Spanish hills. Where else could they have been buried so close to both the countries they loved?

Shifting on my rock till I was sitting comfortably, I felt glad to be there—glad to feel the faint presence of my mother and father, who seemed gradually to discard family legends and the speculations of their children that had wrapped them in layer after layer until they had become unrecognizable. Now they became simply the people they once were. I saw the purposeful way my father walked and the determined line of my mother's jaw, the joy with which he turned a sailboat into the wind, and the lines around her eyes when she listened to a Bach fugue.

I hesitated for a while, fighting the embarrassment I always feel in the presence of ritual, and tempted to rush through our little ceremony just to get it over with. It crossed my mind that if this were a movie, it would end right here at the grave. But that would be Hollywood, and this was real life.

After a while, I lit the candle we had brought with us inside a jar. Then Ruth read aloud the questions we had written down. I took my time, not having rehearsed my responses. Trying not to feel silly, I articulated the things I was sorry for. Mostly they were sins of omission: a lack of sympathy manifest as an absence of kindness to my mother; a blindness to the very existence of my father's feelings.

Then I told them who I had become—the things that would have pleased them, as well as those which would have been difficult. I told them about my life with Ruth, asserting in the face of their silent disapproval, that it was good and true, and that it would last—as, indeed, it has. I talked of being a writer, urging, in the face of their vast indifference, that my father not worry about my finances and that my mother be proud—as I knew she would have been, had she been alive.

It was then that the tears came—the first uncomplicated tears I had shed since the accident. Standing beside the headstone, the simple fact I had been so afraid to face settled there beside me: I missed my parents. I missed them and that was all.

EPILOGUE

$\mathcal{L}ifesaving$

I ONCE EARNED A LIFESAVING medal—a bronze one. Even though bronze is the lowest level, I always thought I could save a drowning person if I had to. I got the medal when I was in the Lower Fifth at St. Mary's Hall. I think silver was the next one up, but I never thought of getting another one. I doubt anyone did—we just took lifesaving for one term and got the bronze.

To pass the test you had to swim thirty-six lengths of the pool on your front and thirty-six on your back. This took me considerable time since I wasn't good at the crawl and preferred the breaststroke. You couldn't take too long, though, since the swim was timed and if you went over the limit you didn't pass.

I practiced a lot for that test, walking down the tamarisk path to Black Rock pool after school and swimming doggedly up and down in the icy water. It was an open-air pool, unheated, just a few yards from the beach. As you went in through the turnstile, there was an enormous thermometer on the wall, which usually indicated that the water temperature was 56 or maybe 62. In high summer, when it reached the seventies, our gym teacher, Mrs. Eggleton (known to everyone as Eggy), made us go in the sea instead. I suppose it saved money for the sports department.

We never practiced our lifesaving in the ocean, which, if you think about it, was a large omission. Thirty-six lengths on your front in a flat, blue pool—even a freezing cold one—hardly replicates the skills needed for saving a life at sea. What about those Atlantic rollers? Even in calm weather they could be fifteen or twenty feet high. What would it be like to swim up one of those liquid mountains, crest the summit and plummet down into the vast pit of swirling black water, before scaling the next one? Is that what my parents tried to do when they found themselves in the ocean, the suction of the burning ship threatening to slam them against the hull over and over?

In fact, they may well have died of the cold before they even contemplated swimming off into the dark. Sometime after the accident, I read in a newspaper that women were more likely to die of hypothermia because they wore skimpier clothing and that some from the *Lakonia* drowned wearing evening dress. In any case, I can't see them setting out to swim purposefully towards—towards what? Could they have seen the rescue ships once they were down in those swells?

Lifesaving class didn't teach us how to cope with currents either. Black Rock pool had no disturbance more serious than the churning of the intake pipe, which we all avoided since it brought freezing water straight from the ocean just the other side of the wall. If you swam in a straight line from the diving board to the steps at the shallow end, nothing pulled you off course. In the ocean, though, you could head for a point that you fixed your eyes on—a tree, say, on the edge of a cliff, or a boat anchored a mile away—but however hard you swam, you might end up ten miles down-current. Even swimming in the surf off Brighton beach with Eggy yelling instructions from the shore, some of us drifted half a mile down towards the pier. I had heard of people who swam towards Lands End and ended up on the Isle of Wight. Or something like that. In the Atlantic, with no land in sight, the currents might take you towards a waiting rescue ship, or simply pull you in the opposite direction until finally you rolled over and felt the ocean pouring into your nose and mouth, pressing in on your ears and filling all your cavities till you became just another piece of flotsam riding the swift current away from the ship.

The backstroke part of the test was difficult because you couldn't see where you were going. When I was thirteen, every evening after school I practiced looking down the length of my body and fixing my eyes on a point I was swimming away from, resisting the urge to twist myself around to see what lay ahead. In the pool, you could always crack your head on the end wall if you forgot to calculate the distance. In the ocean, the obstacles would be more unpredictable: driftwood? Sharks? Debris from the shipwreck that dumped you there in the first place?

YOU couldn't get your lifesaving medal without diving to the bottom. Eggy never said this was to pull up a body that had gone down for the third time. Instead, it was presented as a skill to retrieve small objects.

We dived for coins mostly. I practiced with pennies and shillings, or sometimes a sixpence, which was small and shiny enough to be virtually invisible.

Uptailing like a duck, I would flip my feet in the air and dive straight down. Then I would run the palms of my hands over the concrete bottom of the pool, a little stream of bubbles escaping from my nose and chlorine scratching my eyeballs, which would be bloodshot and weeping after an afternoon of searching for sixpences. But I always found the coin: I was good at this part of lifesaving.

I knew the ocean was deep out there, mid-Atlantic, that divers got the bends when they came up too fast and that people sometimes went down in compression chambers. But how deep was deep? Anyway, what would you dive for out there? A lost handbag? A missing shoe?

Long after those numb years in Spain, when finally I began to think about the accident, I couldn't stop wondering what I would have done if I had been there—and I might well have been, since I had very nearly accepted my parents' invitation to go with them on the cruise. I was sure I would have saved them: I would have gone down the ladder with them and kept them alive by force of will, shouting at them to keep swimming, grabbing a lifejacket or a floating door, commandeering a raft. Deep inside, I suspected that I should have been there—that I'd had no right to stay behind.

I never obsessed about whether I could have persuaded them into a lifeboat. I was too young to picture myself taking charge; my parents, even dead, remained all-powerful in the way that parents seem to children. The very idea of cajoling my father into anything was absurd, and my mother would never have listened to my arguments as long as he was rushing around, getting in the way. Besides, as a script it lacked drama—and drama was necessary to combat the guilt. So I dwelt, instead, on the possibilities of the struggle to stay alive in the ocean.

I could have kept my mother afloat; we had learned how to do that in lifesaving class. We memorized a number of moves to knock away a drowning person when they grabbed us as we were told a drowning person always does. These were stylized moves like a karate set, which we practiced in pairs on land, the saver blocking the drowner's grab with a forearm and then spinning the poor, panicked girl around and locking her into one of the two towing grips. You had to swim on your back to tow the drowner, with your arms underneath hers and your hands locked together over her chest. She would be on her back too, above you, pressing you under water unless you swam very hard with your legs, which were all you had to keep both of you afloat. Alternatively, you could hold her head pressed between your hands, squashing her ears flat underneath her rubber swimming cap, and tow her that way, which kept her from pushing you under, but left her arms free so she might grasp you at any moment. The head tow was recommended for unconscious drowners, who were less dangerous than conscious ones.

We also learned how to knock out a drowner if she panicked. A solid punch to the jaw, a quick flip of her body onto its back, and the long tow to shore. Of course we didn't really knock out our partners; we acted it out, the saver throwing a Wyatt Earp-like blow in the direction of the drowner's chin, the drowner jerking her head back and going limp. It seemed simple on dry land, but the first time I tried it in the water, I threw my punch and sank like a stone.

The major goal of all drowners, I learned, was to drown you

before you could save them. Saving your own life was the most important thing.

My father would surely have struggled. The question is, would I have been able to punch him in the jaw? Lord knows, I had wanted to often enough through those teenage years when he and I struggled for my mother's attention. I hadn't exactly pictured myself hitting him—hadn't even used words as a weapon between us, being firmly locked into that powerless anger that causes teenagers to sulk, pout, and deny the fury within which they exist for a while. My father seemed no more anxious than I to acknowledge his hostility. "Tell the girl to get up," he would say to my mother crossly, when I lay in bed on the weekend, and: "Is she going to waste away her whole life?" loudly and clearly near the door to my room, but never to my face. It was as if he was as afraid of confronting me as I was of challenging him.

What happened, I wonder, between the years when we would go fishing together at Posingworth Park and those later years when we avoided eye contact and slammed doors as a way of communicating? I remember being excited as we set off early in the morning, just him and me and the dogs. All day, I would row the boat as he directed, stalking the big trout that lurked under the trees near the bank or along the shores of the small, rhododendron-covered island in the middle. I took pride in rowing silently, never splashing an oar, and when we stopped, holding the blades down low to prevent the drips from creating rings that might startle the fish. When we moved off to another part of the lake, I fixed my eye on a beech trunk or a pedestal of the bridge near the boathouse so as to row to the new location in a perfectly straight line. All this, I suppose, to impress my father, who had taught me these things.

My mother, on the other hand, would surely not have needed to be knocked out if I had swum to her aid in those dark waters. She was terrified of the ocean—a candidate for the panicked grab that might have drowned us both, but in my fantasies she put her fear aside and trod water, waiting till I swam my thirty-six lengths to her. Then she cooperated, kicking her legs in tune with mine as I towed her towards Africa.

Sometimes, I tried to picture them during those hours before they left the ship. I imagined my father bustling around when the fire broke out, trying to find out what was going on after the loudspeaker system failed and nobody seemed to be in charge. I saw him speaking to the Greek crew members much as he spoke to Spanish waiters: too loudly and without listening. I saw my mother sitting on a deck bench, wrapped in a blanket, being very quiet. Alternatively, it was my father who was stunned into silence and my mother who took charge, gathering information and bringing it back to him.

As time went by, I read accounts by survivors about those hours of waiting. One of them said that in the middle of the night, after all the lifeboats left, "a curious quiet settled over the ship." Apparently, the remaining hundred and fifty passengers gathered in the Mocambo Room, where someone sat down at the piano and got a group to sing Christmas carols. "Silent Night" floated over the ocean, where survivors drifted and rescue ships converged to snatch the living and the dead from the water. But I couldn't imagine my mother throwing her head back and belting out "The First Noël," and my father had never been known to sing anything. Nor could I really see either of them tucking into the roast duck that had been set out on silver salvers just as the smoke billowed into the ballroom, or politely sharing the cups of tea that were handed around.

Instead, I made up conversations between the two of them, particularly those that took place as time ran out and they realized, as the fire spread and no motor boats were sent from the rescue ships, that soon they'd have to get into the water. Some were bitter: my mother finally turned on my father and told him what a disappointment he'd turned out to be and how she felt she had wasted her life; in others it was my father who was angry, blaming my mother for refusing to get into a lifeboat until it was too late and the boats were all gone. I put into my mother's mouth the outrage that I, myself, felt at my father's insistence on taking a cruise when she had always been so afraid of the sea. And I allowed my father to let rip at last with the barely disguised frustration I had witnessed my whole life. He had forever had to wait around for someone, he stormed: my mother, the children, the chattering women who ambled along with my mother in Spain. And now look where her maddening inability to get a move on had finally landed them.

I also tried out conversations in which they came together in their last hours and talked about their good years together, about us children, about the things for which they were grateful, but I couldn't quite believe in these Hollywood endings, perhaps because I relied on a degree of hostility between my parents for the opportunities it opened up between my mother and me. Our bond had so often, in those last years, depended on the delicious moments when we formed an alliance against my father.

In any case, my understanding of the two of them was too limited for me to create a credible story. At nineteen, I knew them only in terms of myself as their daughter—not in the larger way that an adult child gets to know a parent. The truth was that I couldn't see them clearly and that now I never would. All I had left were isolated memories, like a collection of snapshots I still have to this day.

There are pictures of my mother at the piano while my sister and I play viola and clarinet; her glasses slip down her nose as she peers up at the music and down at the keys; she fumbles through a difficult passage with a heap of wrong notes and yells *Damn!* but we all press ahead until we're so uncoordinated that we break into laughter. There is my father, with his head under the hood of the car, compulsively polishing the engine, and my mother lying in a striped deck chair on the stone patio outside the living room. She is there when I come home from school on a hot day in early summer, her arms stretched out on the wooden armrests, hands turned up to the sun as if she can never absorb enough of the good stuff. Her face, already nut brown, looks like the face of someone I don't know, and when I talk to her, she murmurs back at me as if from a dream. There are, too, images of both of them in Spain: Mother standing on the sea front in Caldetas in her long, towelling robe, white with red dots, and an air mattress under her arm, or leaning down to talk animatedly in Catalan with Pedro, the one-armed car-park attendant; Pa at the bowling alley, a little removed but smiling benignly at a crowd of family and friends.

There are some pictures, though, that I try not to look at: a depressed woman sitting alone in a wing chair listening to Mahler with a gin and tonic in her hand; a man's tight lips and set jaw as he drives us to a vacation, speeding relentlessly all day to keep up with his schedule. And then there's my mother's back as she disappears through the door, walking out on my father and me with the dreaded words: "If you two don't stop fighting, I'm leaving for good." These I have thrown into the darkness of memory's compost heap from which they emerge now and then, like flowers or weeds—I'm never quite sure which.

IN lifesaving class, we learned how to get the water out of our drowners once we had dragged them ashore, and how to get them breathing again, although this was before the days of mouth-to-mouth. Kneeling beside our prone partner, we would press both hands down on her lungs, counting aloud in a rhythm shouted out by Eggy. Then we slid our hands up to her shoulders and down her upper arms to lift her head up, encouraging the air to enter. I never thought of real people needing these services, least of all my parents. After all, they could both swim quite well.

My father had an efficient crawl. On the beach in Spain, he would stand up in his baggy black trunks, his long, white legs like sticks, and run straight down the beach to dive through the first wave. Then he would swim very fast on some predetermined route, often taking in anchored sailboats and colored buoys along the way. When he came out, he liked to shake himself close to somebody's sunbaked body, feigning ignorance when the sunbather swore at him.

My mother swam cautiously. In deep water she looked like a large dog as she lifted her head high out of the water and moved forward with a steady breaststroke. Like a comfortable barge, she pressed ahead with no bobbing and no splashing, although she was not averse to playing in the surf. Sometimes she would let herself be flung up the beach with the little breakers, her legs flying into the air, her head thrown back. She shouted and laughed, then staggered up the beach, tugging the elastic swimsuit away from her legs to let the sand fall out.

At Black Rock nobody ever mentioned that a drowner could die. Nobody suggested that someone might drown far away before we got there, or before we even knew she needed our help. If drowning were to occur in our lives, it would be in a tiled pool; we would have our swimsuits on; we would knock her out no matter how hard she tried to hang on to us, we would tow her to dry land, and then we would jump-start her breathing.

I SPENT years trying to picture my parents leaving the burning ship, but I was stuck with a bird's-eye view of their small figures on the deck. Sometimes I glimpsed a close-up of my mother putting her foot on the first rung of the ladder that led over the side but I always drew back. For years and years her foot hovered over that top rung, as if held on perpetual pause, while I did everything I could to avoid feeling the icy water creeping up my legs as her feet groped for the rungs below.

It took a scene from a movie I saw to shake me loose from my distant observation post. As it happened, *The Black Stallion* was playing over the Christmas holiday—always a difficult time, with its lurking memories of 1963—and, arriving a bit late, I found myself sitting in the second row. A few minutes into the film, the ship with the equine hero on board caught fire. I squirmed down lower into my seat, watching as the camera took in the flames and the passengers' panic. Soon, after much struggling and sweating, with his nostrils flaring and his panicked eyes showing white, the savvy horse broke loose and leapt into the sea. From then on, the scene was shot from the point of view of someone who was floating in the ocean.

Shivering uncontrollably, I found myself there in the water

looking up, the angle accentuated by my seat location almost at the foot of the big screen. Little plumes of water broke next to the camera, whose eye rose and fell with the waves, and the ship, a fiery light in the darkness, grew gradually more distant. I felt profoundly shaken, bobbing in the oily swell along with the camera.

For years I had avoided backing down with my mother into that awful mass of water. I hadn't felt my mother's clothes bind themselves around my kicking legs as her shoes fell away from my feet and started their slow, twirling journey to the bottom of the Atlantic. I had never splashed away into the darkness with her, losing sight of the others who were abandoning ship. I had never struggled away from the blaze of light, a briny taste in my nose and mouth, and the numbing cold working its way into the center of my body until the ship was a distant mass of smoke and flame, the lights of its Christmas tree still bright on the upper deck while its guardrails melted in the heat.

But once I had gone down those swaying steps, I could no longer hold on to the fantasy of saving my parents. It had worked only as long as I saw the *Lakonia* from high in the sky— as long as I remained insulated from acrid smoke, leaping flames, and the ladder that was more than just a top rung. I knew at last the awful power of the water I would have encountered—the water that engulfed the two of them, stopping both their watches, and perhaps their hearts, at the same moment.

JUDITH BARRINGTON is an Anglo-American poet and memoirist, author of two volumes of poetry, *Trying to Be an Honest Woman* (1985) and *History and Geography* (1989), and *Writing the Memoir: From Truth to Art* (1997). She is the editor of *An Intimate Wilderness: Lesbian Writers on Sexuality* (1991).

Barrington's work has been included in numerous anthologies, including *The Stories That Shape Us: Twenty Women Write About the West*, *A Formal Feeling Comes*, *From Here We Speak: An Anthology of Oregon Poetry*, and *Hers 3*. Her work has been published in many literary journals, including *Americas Review*, *Kenyon Review*, *ZYZZYVA*, *The American Voice*, *Poetry London*, *13th Moon*, *The GSU Review*, and *The Chattahoochee Review*.

Her awards include the Andrés Berger Award, the Dulwich Festival International Poetry Contest, and the Stewart H. Holbrook Award for outstanding contributions to Oregon's literary life. She is the founder of Flight of the Mind Writing Workshops and lives in Portland, Oregon.

colophon

 This book was designed by Marcia Barrentine. The cover is set in Ribbon and Frutiger; the text is set in Palatino. The front cover photograph is of the author's parents, Rex and Violet Barrington, taken in the mid-fifties. The photograph on the back cover is of the author with her father, in *Guapa*'s collapsible dinghy in Shoreham Harbor around 1956. Also on the back cover is the painting *La Riera* by Joan Barrington, which depicts a scene in Caldetas. Except where noted, all graphics are used by permission of Judith Barrington.

The photographs in the text were taken at or near the time of the events described in *Lifesaving*.

Page 13: Yacht race off Shoreham, England

Page 27: The author and her Triumph at the border between France and Spain

Page 39: Perelada Castle, Perelada, Spain

Page 55: The cafés on the *rambla* in front of the Hotel Paris, Figueras, Spain

Page 65: Village street, Spain

Page 75: Street scene with the Hotel Paris, Figueras, Spain

Page 91: Room at the Hotel Paris, Figueras, Spain